This Pats Year

A Trek through a Season as a Football Fan

Sean Glennon

Taylor Trade Publishing

Lanham • New York • Dallas • Boulder • Toronto • Oxford

Published by Taylor Trade Publishing
An imprint of The Rowman & Littlefield Publishing Group, Inc.
4501 Forbes Boulevard, Suite 200
Lanham, Maryland 20706

Distributed by National Book Network

Library of Congress Cataloging-in-Publication Data

Glennon, Sean, 1966–
  This Pats year : a trek through a season as a football fan /
Sean Glennon.—1st Taylor Trade Pub. ed.
    p. cm.
  ISBN 1-58979-119-3 (cloth : alk. paper)
  1. New England Patriots (Football team)—History—Chronology.
2. Football fans—United States—Anecdotes. I. Title.
  GV956.N36G54 2004
  796.332'64'0974461—dc22

                                                    2004003550

Manufactured in the United States of America.

To Seamus and Mo, who are everything.

1/23/03

Contents

Acknowledgments

It's hard to figure out where to begin thanking my wife, Maureen Turner, for her help with this book. I guess her direct involvement with the writing process is a good starting point. *This Pats Year* has benefited from the work of a number of talented editors, and Mo is one of them. Mo, who is a remarkably talented journalist, was the first to read the book versions of my game-day narratives. She made a great number of excellent suggestions, all of which helped me tell better, more complete stories. I'll never stop owing her for that. But that's not nearly the whole of it. Mo has provided support and validation throughout the long process of writing this book. Mo was the person who kept me from giving up over the slow months I spent working to sell the concept for the newspaper column on which this book is based. She was the person who was left to work on our home improvement projects alone as I went off on my adventures every Sunday for four months. She was the person who told me repeatedly that I could finish this book. And she was the person who took on the lion's share of parenting duties during our son's first three months, while I was working on the manuscript.

I also need to thank my son, Seamus, for being so understanding about the long hours his daddy needed to put in on this project. You really are an excellent baby, Seamus.

This Pats Year is based on a series of narrative essays originally published in the *Boston Phoenix*. Many thanks to the *Phoenix* for giving an oddball concept a shot. Thanks, specifically, to *Phoenix* news editor Susan Ryan-Vollmar, who helped shape the column, and copy editors Suzanne Bashoff and Catherine Tumber, who, along with Susan, made me look like a better writer than I am. And thanks to the Phoenix Newspaper Group's Senior Managing Editor Clif Garboden, without whose help I'm sure I never would have got the *Phoenix* to give the column the nod in the first place. Thanks, also, to Salon.com, which published my narrative about watching the Patriots-Raiders conference play-off game in January 2002. The *Phoenix* series was inspired by that piece.

My friends Don Fluckinger and Dean Chadwin provided an amazing amount of encouragement and some crucial advice regarding both the *Phoenix* series and the process involved in turning it into a book. Don also accompanied me on my road trips to Manhattan and Buffalo. And for the latter trip, he deserves something akin to a Purple Heart. Tom Shea and Suzanne Strempek Shea provided the connection to my agent, John Talbot. And John, of course, worked hard to sell the book concept.

Michael Emmerich and Taylor Publishing got what I was trying to do and made the book happen. Michael, Stephen Driver, and Steven Long worked to make my narratives stronger and my language clearer.

And, of course, none of this would have been possible without the help of the friends and family (and a few complete strangers) who offered advice, provided ideas, hooked me up with fan acquaintances, hit the road with me, and invited me into their homes (and their buses) on game days. They are Tom Vannah, Kyle Provost, John Maher, Betsy Mears, David Crescenzi, Shannon Ryan, John Reis, Darby O'Brien, Gainer O'Brien, Nic Facendola, Chris Glennon, Tom Chisholm, Bob DeMaria, Dave Niro, Chris Abbiuso, Keith Gentili, Julie Glennon, Tom Glennon, Pat Glennon, Kim Shulman, David Shulman, Ardath Garfield, Vera Colleary, Deb Colleary, Max Germer, Ken Powers, and Stacey James. A few others whose contributions were indirect but nonetheless vital: Ken and Laura DeCoste, David Daley, and William Feinstein.

And since no one ever learned to write all on his own, I feel obliged to thank the teachers, the librarians, the bookstore clerks, the friends who've recommended books, my folks, my wife, and everyone who ever got me reading, kept me reading, or encouraged me to write. A few specific teachers whom it wouldn't be right not to mention by name: Jose Vieira, who didn't let kids like me get lost in the system; Nancy Iannitelli, Joanne Crescenzi, and

David Lenson, who told me I needed to keep writing; Ken Gibbs, who taught me that writing is a process; and Robert Walker, who insisted on teaching me to be a journalist even though I made it clear I didn't want to learn.

Note: The characters and events in this book are real. Some of the names have been changed.

Prologue

As it turns out, even heartbreak is somehow more noticeable in its absence.

That odd fact became clear to me just about halfway through my late-night drive across Massachusetts February 3, 2002.

I was on my way home to the western Mass city of Northampton from Milford, the old mill town in central Mass where I grew up and where I'd just spent the evening with old friends watching the New England Patriots win Super Bowl XXXVI. It was the Pats' first win in three visits to the NFL championship game, and for all I knew at the time it might have been the only Super Bowl win the team would ever get.

As I drove out of the Worcester rest stop on the Massachusetts Turnpike, muddy, too-hot coffee assaulting my tongue and throat, the weird truth just sort of came on. Not like some kind of epiphany, mind you. Not like some great, life-changing realization. It slipped over me as softly and gently as daybreak, then just sort of lay there as if it were exactly what I ought to have expected, as if it were something I'd always known but hadn't ever needed to think about.

The weird feeling that had been riding with me for the previous 40 minutes—and that I suspect had been around for much longer than that, maybe from the moment Adam Vinatieri's game-winning field goal cut through the uprights hours earlier—was the absence of the letdown I'd been preparing to experience for most of a week. The heartbreak that had been part and parcel of being a Boston-area sports fan at least since the Celtics fell on hard times shortly after winning their last NBA championship in '85, and probably longer, probably since 1918, had blown town, if only temporarily. And though I never, ever would have expected it, I kind of missed that feeling. I caught myself kind of yearning for disappointment.

* * *

The really crazy thing is that I've spent much of my life working hard to distance myself from that very feeling, to avoid that
very defining experience of sports fandom in my part of the country. I'm not a big fan of heartbreak or of frustration, so I've tried
not to be a fan of Boston-area sports teams.

I'm not a Red Sox fan. I never have been.

The truth of the matter is that I'm not a fan of any baseball
team. And I have a good idea that's because of the Sox.

It wouldn't feel right to root for any team except the Red Sox.
I can remember as a kid, heading out with my dad, brother, and
sister to visit my grandfather. We'd find him, as often as not, sitting by his kitchen window watching the Sox on his little black-
and-white TV. And when I think of the Sox, when I think of Sox
fans, I think of my grandfather in that window at the side of a
farmhouse that burned down more than a decade ago. You simply
can't betray that kind of memory. But I also can't handle the idea
of backing a team that's guaranteed to tear my heart out every
single year. I just don't have the strength for it.

On a handful of occasions over the last three decades—when it
seemed like the Sox's moment simply had to be at hand—I've
fallen into the trap of believing, in spite of everything experience
has taught me. I've never quite jumped on the bandwagon, never
called myself a fan, but I've reached the point of thinking, "Good
for them. The good old Sox are finally gonna get theirs." And, of
course, I've foolishly allowed myself to become excited about seeing it.

This, of course, is how the Sox get even the toughest of us.
This is why everyone in Massachusetts, not just the real diehard
Sox fans, still spits three times to ward off evil spirits at the mention of the name Bill Buckner. This is what reminds those of us
who can't invest ourselves in a team like the Red Sox of just what
it is that makes Sox fans so sadly, tragically admirable.

I used to follow the Celtics closely. In fact, there was a time
back in the days of Bird, McHale, and Parish when I'd rarely miss
a game. Then Len Bias died. And things just got uglier from there.
I still watch a few games every season. I still hope Red will find a
way to bring back the glory days. But I can't entrust my emotional and spiritual well-being to that team.

I haven't attended a Cs game since before the team moved out of Boston Garden.

The last time I was at a Bruins game, Bobby Orr and Phil Esposito were on the ice. I've watched a play-off game or two in the 32 years since the Bs captured their last Stanley Cup, but most years I could hardly name more than two or three starters.

My relationship with the Patriots has been a good deal more complicated than my relationships with the other local teams.

It's only natural. The Pats are, after all, the squad that plays what I consider the greatest sport ever invented.

I've been an NFL fan for as long as I can remember. I remember being part of an awe-filled conversation about Franco Harris at a friend's seventh birthday party—almost a year after the Immaculate Reception (a play I was too young to remember seeing when it happened, but that I was aware of by the time I turned seven). I remember playing tackle ball in Billy Atherton's backyard in the early '70s, with whatever kid was quarterbacking on a given play calling the cadence, "Griese says hut" (rendered thus: "GrEE-SEE says HUT"). I remember the excitement that swept through Milford when Howie Long, who'd played for the Milford High School Scarlet Hawks, was drafted to play for the Oakland Raiders.

And my passion for football has never diminished. In fact, it only grows more intense with every season. I can watch any game between any two NFL teams and not only be entertained, but become animated and emotionally invested in the outcome. I start counting weeks until the start of the next season the day after the Super Bowl. I'm as careful to keep my schedule clear on draft day as I am to keep game days uncluttered. I look for reasons to sneak away from the dinner table to keep up with the scores on Thanksgiving.

Yet, through a life as a football fan, a life in which I've never lived outside of New England, I'd never been an honest-to-God Patriots fan.

The truth of the matter is that I'm a Raiders fan, and have been since I was a kid. And in many ways, I became a Raiders fan as a reaction to the Patriots of the '70s.

It would be a disservice to the word "bad" to say the Patriots of my childhood were a bad football team. The Pats of that era were more than bad—they were aggressively awful, possessed, it seemed to me at the time, of a burning desire to lose. They were a team plagued by unfit ownership and inept management, a team like the modern-day Cincinnati Bengals or Detroit Lions, run by an organization that seemed determined to make the wrong decisions. They drafted poorly most years. And on those odd occasions when they drafted well, it didn't matter anyhow. The team's best players never had the support they needed to thrive.

There were those players who excelled in spite of the Patriots' constant quest for inadequacy—Steve Grogan, Sam "Bam" Cunningham, Stanley Morgan, Russ Francis—but they were few and painfully far between.

The adult Pats fans I knew as a kid weren't like adult Sox fans. They didn't express hope at the start of each season. They didn't get truly excited after a key win or two. They never expected anything other than failure or, at the very best, limited success followed by complete collapse.

I latched onto the team that was, in my estimation, most unlike the Pats. The Raiders were a team constantly searching for ways to win. Where the Pats would do nothing to help themselves, the Raiders would do anything. They were branded dirty, a team of cheap-shot artists. (This was never more true in any place than it was in New England in 1977 after the famously nasty Raiders defensive back Art Tatum delivered a hit that crippled young Patriots wide receiver Darryl Stingley—an event many New England fans still have neither forgotten nor forgiven the Raiders for.) They were booed wherever they went. And they didn't care.

The Raiders didn't care about what was said about them, because they didn't have to. They won football games. They won championships. I liked that.

It didn't matter that the Raiders would go years between championships, either. I didn't need to back a dynasty. I didn't need to be a Cowboys fan. I only needed to know that my team was in the hunt, that it was hungry, that players, coach, and owner alike were interested first and foremost in doing what it took to win. You always knew that with the Raiders. Just like you always knew with the Pats that whatever might be right, there would always be just enough wrong that things would ultimately fall apart.

The Patriots weren't a sad-sack bunch of perpetual also-rans, like the Sox or the late '80s/early '90s–era Buffalo Bills. They weren't even a group of lovable losers, like the Chicago Cubs or the pre-Gruden Tampa Bay Buccaneers. They were a team you could only ever look at through your fingers.

I've never rooted against the Patriots. In fact, I've always sort of held a little place in my heart for them.

Milford is only a handful of exits up Interstate 495 from Foxborough, where the Pats play, and there has always been a part of me that wanted to be able to take some pride in the team next door. But up through the start of the 2003–04 season, there had never come an early September that found me believing the Patriots would still be playing in late January.

And through the end of the 2001–02 season, there had never been a moment when I truly believed the Patriots would win a Super Bowl. There came a moment when I had to believe they had won a championship—when the scoreboard read Patriots 20, Rams 17 and the game clock read 00:00—but even that moment was separated from one in which I was sure something would get in the way only by a few blinking seconds of utter uncertainty, a few seconds in which there was no telling the real from the imagined.

I never believed the Pats had a chance against the Bears in Super Bowl XX back in '86 (and, of course, neither did anyone anywhere in America). I never thought they'd pull it off against Green Bay in '97, though I certainly knew my fair share of people who did believe the team's moment had finally arrived heading into Super Bowl XXXI, a game the Pats finally lost by two touchdowns.

Even in that weird instant in '02, when Vinatieri's 48-yard field goal put the team up for good as the final seconds ran off the clock (the first time a Super Bowl was ever decided on the last play), when it became undeniably obvious to the logical, reasonable football-watching world that the Pats really were going to earn the Vince Lombardi trophy, there was still a part of me—and of everyone I was watching with; probably of every football fan in New England—that felt a certain familiar, almost unspeakable dread. There was an undeniable part of me that simply expected something to go wrong, even at perhaps the first significant moment in

Patriots history when it absolutely couldn't. A late yellow flag
would sail though the air signaling the start of events that would
wipe out the field goal and send the game to an overtime the Pats
could only lose. The officials would put a second back on the
clock, necessitating a kickoff that would be returned for a game-
winning touchdown. Or maybe it would require direct, history-
altering intervention of some unkind deity. It didn't matter what it
might be. What was important was the notion that if ever a team
were going to lose when losing had been rendered impossible, it
would be the Patriots.

Then a long moment passed. And in New Orleans, a celebration on the field began. And in a little living room in Milford,
Massachusetts, a group of men and women in their mid-30s
looked around at one another with expressions of joyful puzzlement. And across New England rooms full of men and women
looked at each other unconvinced that what they'd just seen wasn't
part of some cruel, teasing dream.

Somehow, the thing no one had ever honestly anticipated had
come to pass. And it was . . . well, it was just plain weird.

I don't know what followed that odd moment elsewhere, but in
the living room at my friend Bob's house on Otis Street in Milford, we celebrated loudly for a while. We screamed and hooted.
We jumped up and high-fived. We pumped our fists and danced.
We held our heads and closed our eyes and took in the moment.
Then we talked about '86 and '97. Some of us talked about how
we'd never thought it would happen. Others talked about how
they'd believed all along. Someone somewhere in the group probably really had believed, too. But there's a difference between belief and hope, a difference you can't help but understand if you've
followed teams like the Red Sox and the Patriots.

There have always been those—the young and the willfully
naive, for the most part—who honestly believe. But there are others, tens or hundreds of thousands of others, who were willing to
allow ourselves a measure of hope even in the utter absence of belief. It was that hopeless hope that set us up to take the fall right
along with the true believers. But in early February 2002, it was
that same hopeless hope that led us to share with the believers
(honest and revisionist alike) the odd sensation of being lifted

rather than falling. It's hard to know what to do with that feeling when it's been the better part of two decades since you've felt it.

After a fairly short while, we started to head for the door. Super Bowls start and end late. Some of us had long drives ahead of us. Others had spouses and kids to get home to. Most of us were just plain worn out. It had been a long, emotionally exhausting day and even if it had somehow come out all right, it had reached the point at which it needed to end.

I drove through downtown Milford, then out past the playing fields where the town dump used to be, past the cemetery and the Wendy's restaurant next to it, and onto I-495, all the while feeling nothing but the disbelief-tinged giddiness that comes standard on those odd occasions when something wonderful comes at you out of nowhere.

I tried reminding myself that there was no real reason for me to be so happy. I wasn't even a Patriots fan. I didn't even care about the Pats. I wouldn't have been upset if they'd lost, so how could I be so delighted that they'd won? None of it took. It did mean something to me that the Patriots had won that game. And the question of whether it should have, while sort of philosophically interesting, was practically irrelevant. Besides, it serves no purpose to go around questioning the things in life that make you feel good, particularly the innocent ones, so I decided to ride with the emotion, knowing it would be temporary either way.

I never really tried to get a handle on the other feeling that had been poking at me softly. It was still only vaguely noticeable at the time. It didn't yet rate investigation.

But it continued to nudge me with increasing vigor as I made my way up I-495 and onto the Pike. And by the time I pulled into the Worcester rest stop, thinking a cup of coffee might come in handy for the long drive still ahead, it had become rather a nuisance.

Ten minutes later, the moment came at which I finally recognized the odd, niggling sensation as a longing for heartbreak. I didn't need the coffee so much after that.

As I drove the long stretch of highway between Worcester and Sturbridge, and the even longer one between Sturbridge and Palmer,

I got to thinking about how losing, and the expectation of losing, even when it stands in direct opposition to stubborn hope, can't simply be one of the defining aspects of Boston-area sports fandom. Neither, I decided, was it likely an experience shared by a relative few—the purview of Red Sox, Cubs, and L.A. Clippers fans. It had to be universal, or at the very least nearly so, excepting only those fortunate enough to witness a dynasty, and even then only during their team's term of greatness. Celtics fans up until '85, say. Or Chicago Bulls fans during the Jordan era. Only Yankees fans, it seemed to me, could really be considered even semipermanently exempt from the sensation of simply knowing their team is destined to lose.

Only one team can win the championship in any given sport in any given season, which means there's always substantially more disappointment than elation to go around. And while it's tempting to think a team like the Red Sox, which typically plays well enough through most seasons to at least allow hope, sets its fans up for more heartbreak than the perpetually miserable likes of the Cincinnati Bengals, I became not so sure.

Disappointment, like every other emotional experience, comes in a variety of nuanced forms. But however it comes, whether it burns, envelops, hovers and drops, or simply lingers endlessly, it's disappointment just the same.

What struck me as truly remarkable, though, is the fact that sports fans, in large part, are so much better at accepting heartbreak than I've ever been. My grandfather wasn't the only person I've ever known who stuck with the Sox year in and year out despite the readily apparent fact that the team can sometimes get close, but can't ever close the deal. And I've known people all my life who stuck with the Pats, watching them mostly lose season after endless season, knowing most Septembers that their team's season would end with a whimper in December, knowing, in fact, that the Pats would be out of play-off contention by no later than early November.

Indeed, given that the bulk of sports fans remain loyal to their home teams regardless of the teams' successes or failures, it seemed to me that I must be missing something more profound and important than a temporary sense of heartache.

* * *

By the time I got off the Pike at Exit 4, heading north on Interstate 91 toward home, I had decided that I needed to go looking for the thing I was missing, the thing that makes a fan a homer. And I knew that the only way I was going to find what I was looking for was to experience what real fans of the home team experience.

Everything I knew about Pats fans already, I knew from spending time with them—with the fans I'd grown up with, the ones I'd watched the Super Bowl with, and the ones I'd encountered along the way. I realized the way to learn more, to discover what makes a fan—of the Pats, of sports, of anything—was to branch out, to find fans I didn't know, fans whose experiences were far removed from my own in some cases, and watch them being themselves— or, better still, take part in their game-day activities.

I decided what I needed to do was to spend a full season hanging out with Pats fans—strange and familiar—to learn what I could from the experience. And I decided the best time to do that was in the season following the team's best ever, a season that had ended with a largely unexpected victory in the league's championship game. I would be out among the Pats faithful at a time when they expected, perhaps hoped for, more than usual. And whether Pats fans ultimately got another championship or something substantially less in the 2002 season, I'd get to spend time with them in a rare period in which anything truly would seem possible.

I also wanted to see if a season of concentrated time with fans of the NFL club that had always been my home team would end up transforming me. I wanted to see if being with the fans would turn me into one. I didn't think anything could move me off my Raiders. But I'd just watched the Patriots win a Super Bowl; I was no longer willing to rule anything out.

What follow are the stories of a football season as experienced by the fans of one team. Some of the stories have happy endings. Others don't. Some of the stories are sweet. Others are bitter. Many defy the imagination. Ultimately, these are nothing more than the stories of what I did with my game days. None of them are going to change the world. But what I did with my game days in the fall of 2002 was spend time with an assortment of fascinating and real people. Not all of them were likable. Not all of them were comprehensible. But they were all damned interesting.

I'm still not sure the experience answered my every question about what it is to be a fan or what makes a home-team loyalist. But they might have. I suspect that all the answers are in these stories somewhere. It's just a matter of uncovering them.

What I do know for certain now is that there's something meaningful about caring—about a sports team or about an opera singer, it really doesn't matter what. I know, that is, that there's value in the very state of fandom, in the very act of believing in spite of logic and of allowing something to have meaning and weight in your life even knowing it might end up hurting. And I've become confident, for the first time in my life, in the notion that sometimes believing in something, even at the times when believing makes no sense at all, has a value and a power all its own.

1.

Game 1 vs. Pittsburgh Steelers

Monday, September 9, 2002

Record 0–0

There are 68,000 people at Gillette Stadium tonight. We are not them.

We're not far from the brand new stadium. Less than two miles away, in fact. But less than two miles away still isn't eye-level seats on the 50 yard line. It isn't even the remotest, thin-air corner of the upper deck.

Less than two miles from the stadium is still most of two miles away from the action. And it sure as hell isn't where anyone dreamed of being on this night.

We're gathered in a bar called the End Zone, which sits just down Route 1 from Gillette. And most of us are not happy about it.

We are the dispossessed, disappointed, and disgruntled. Some of us are greedy. Some are opportunistic. Some are probably greedy and opportunistic. Most of us are drunk or well on our way to it. And nearly everyone in the place is largely out of luck. The simple fact is that most of the people here would rather be in the stadium.

There's something amazing happening here in Foxborough tonight. More than one amazing thing, really.

To begin with, it's the first Monday night of the 2002 NFL season. And that alone brings on a couple different types of energy. There's the energy that derives naturally from the fact that it's the tail end of the league's opening weekend, an energy built up in football fans over the course of the off-season, over the course of months passed without a professional football game—a Christmas Eve kind of anticipatory energy that's in no way specific to this

1

particular game, the NFL, football, or sport. It's the same energy
one can feel on the opening night of a much-anticipated movie or
Broadway play, the same energy that builds up in the lines of kids
and their parents outside bookstores on the day a new *Harry Pot-
ter* book is released, the energy you feel on the way in to the club
on the night your favorite band finally plays in your town.

Then there's the specific energy of this event, the energy that
flows from the understanding that tonight's game between the
New England Patriots and the Pittsburgh Steelers is important,
not only because of what it means to the team, but because the
league and the executives at ABC have identified it as this week's
marquee event. While questions will invariably arise as an NFL
season wears on about the selection of some of the games on the
Monday Night Football schedule, there's rarely any doubt that the
season opener belongs in prime time. And there's certainly no
doubt about whether this matchup deserves a national audience.
The Pats and the Steelers last played in the AFC championship
back in late January, a game that decided which team would represent the conference in Super Bowl XXXVI. The Pats, of course,
won that game, then went on to upset the heavily favored St.
Louis Rams in the biggest event in professional sports.

The rematch between these two teams tonight brings together the
defending league champions and a Steelers team many experts consider a favorite to advance to Super Bowl XXXVII, in January 2003.

There's much more at work than just that, though.

There's also the fact that the Patriots are christening their new
home, Gillette Stadium—reputed to be one of the best facilities in
professional football. That's cause for celebration even among
those of us who aren't lucky enough to be sitting in the stands
tonight. The last time this team played a premiere game in a new
stadium was in '71, the year it changed its name from the Boston
Patriots to the New England Patriots and ended a gypsy decade in
which it played home games at Fenway Park, Boston University
Stadium, Boston College's Alumni Stadium, and finally Harvard
Stadium, with a move into the horrid concrete mistake then
known as Schaefer Stadium (later Sullivan Stadium and, finally,
Foxboro Stadium—spelled with that truncated version of the
town's name for reasons I've never understood). That team was

coming off a 1970 season in which it managed two wins. And though it would improve significantly in '71, that was largely because it had nowhere to go but up. It would finish the 1971 season with a record of 6–8.

In that first year in Foxborough, the second season after the AFL-NFL merger, the Pats were among the least threatening of the combined league's 26 teams. The team's roster that season included just one player who would ever make any significant mark on the NFL. Rookie quarterback Jim Plunkett would earn Super Bowl rings in '81 and '84—as a leader of the Oakland and L.A. Raiders. In his four seasons with the Pats, Plunkett was known mainly as a guy who spent a lot of time on his back.

And it's the same difficult history that includes the complete misuse of Plunkett—plus two major Super Bowl losses (a 46–10 pummeling by the Chicago Bears in '86 and a 35–21 beating by the Green Bay Packers in '97) and as many losing seasons as winning ones—that is the bigger part of what makes this night special.

Tonight, for the first time in their 42-year history, the Patriots are opening a season as defending NFL champs.

The excitement that swept over Pats fans, old and new, seven months ago when the team upended the Rams has only grown more intense during the off-season and preseason. But so, too, has a certain nervousness. Tonight, New England and the rest of football-watching America begins to learn whether the Pats' 20–17 victory in that Super Bowl was the work of a truly great team that had been grossly underestimated going in, or simply a high-profile example of the unwritten rule of football: Any team can beat any other team on any given Sunday.

No one can take away the Vince Lombardi trophy the Patriots brought back from New Orleans in February, but there's still a matter of regional pride on the line. If the Pats don't play the favored Steelers hard tonight, it will look very much like Super Bowl XXXVI was a fluke. And no one wants to believe their heroes just got lucky.

So while almost none of us here at the End Zone tonight are where we'd truly like to be, we're all happy to be here in a larger sense.

In a weird way, I'm happier than most. Or at least I am now that there's a crowd beginning to gather. I drove the better part of 100 miles from Northampton to Foxborough tonight. My friend Kyle and I made the trip without tickets and without real thoughts about getting them. Sure, we'd rather be at the game. There isn't an NFL fan in America who wouldn't choose to be in attendance at a Monday Night Football game if it were possible. But we never thought of it as a possibility. We left western Mass at the end of our workday, six o'clock, figuring that by the time we got to Foxborough, it would be nothing more than a frustrating waste of time even to try to find scalped tickets. We figured if we couldn't be at the game, we could at least be near it.

Kyle and I have been sitting at the corner of the End Zone's bar since about quarter to eight, happy as can be about never having hit traffic on the way out (by the time we reached Route 1, the actual game crowd had been in town tailgating for hours), drinking ale and eating some of the worst bar food ever concocted. Ziti covered in something the End Zone's "special" game-day menu promised would be marinara sauce. It's red but far too sweet and smoky to be marinara. Maybe it's barbecue sauce. Maybe it's ketchup and liquid smoke. Whatever it is, it's awful.

We've had the bar mostly to ourselves during the time we've been here, too. The End Zone is a fairly big place. And while a windowed wall that separates the long L-shaped bar and the area with the dance floor and DJ platform (I'm sure the owners call it a stage) has the effect of making the room seem slightly smaller than it is, the near total emptiness of the place has managed to make us feel a lot like losers just the same. There are, after all, thousands of people gathered just down the road to witness the same event we've come to see. Thousands. Partying in parking lots. Pushing their way toward Gillette and into their seats. Watching the special highlight reel from the Patriots' championship run on a huge Diamond Vision screen. Getting ready for some football, as Hank Williams Jr. would have it.

And then there's Kyle and me, who have just spent a little better than an hour sitting in an all-but-empty bar, waiting to watch the game on whichever of the little bar TVs we can see best from where we're perched. Two guys who call ourselves big football fans, one of us (Kyle), an actual Patriots fan. Stuck in this room with a handful of ticket holders who should have put down their drinks and headed for the stadium long ago. And one loudmouth named Pat.

Pat's a friendly enough guy, but no less of a jackass for it.

A man in his late 30s or maybe his early 40s (but only maybe) with a healthy (if nerdily styled) head of dirty blond hair, Pat wears a Red Sox T-shirt and glasses with frames too big for his face. He says he's originally from Boston but moved to Providence, Rhode Island, several years back. His odd hybrid accent gives all the evidence we might have needed to back up that part of his story.

We get no evidence at all to support the rest of what Pat has to say about himself.

He sits next to us at the bar talking about how easy it would have been for him to get tickets to the game if he'd really wanted them.

He claims he used to own one of those ticket agencies, the kind that are legal in New Hampshire, the kind everyone (except the people who own and operate them) refer to as legal scalpers, because they buy up blocks of seats to sporting events and rock shows, then resell them at absurdly high markups. This detail, without a doubt, is what most puts me off Pat. It's difficult to have respect for those who make their living so blatantly and cynically taking advantage of others.

Pat says he drove up to Foxborough hoping to meet some friends and find tickets to the game. But he didn't meet his friends. And because of that, he lost interest in getting into Gillette, even though he absolutely, definitely could have. He'd rather just go on home.

I spend the better part of the time Pat sits next to me watching the level of his beer drop painfully slowly, sip by sip, and wishing he'd do precisely what he claims to be on the verge of, wishing he'd get out before kickoff comes around and persuades him to stay.

When he finally gets up and says good-bye, I wish him a safe drive back. I really do hope he'll be safe, but I mostly mean, "Please don't change your mind about leaving." He doesn't.

Now it's climbing up on nine. Kickoff is approaching. And over the past few minutes the End Zone has gone from mostly empty to fairly full. It seems that everyone who made it out to Foxborough but didn't manage to find a ticket has found this bar. And while I recognize that those around me may be feeling down on their luck, I'm glad to have them around. A football game requires a crowd, even if it is a crowd of the drunk, downtrodden, and downright strange.

Kelly is well past drunk. She tells me all about how her ticket to tonight's game was stolen. She says she was hopping tailgate parties when it happened. And it would be impossible not to believe her. Young, sandy haired, and just plump enough to be cute without being honestly attractive, she has the look of someone who spent a few evenings at frat parties while she was in college (she may well have been a "little sister" somewhere). As she worked her way through the stadium parking lots, she tells me, someone went into her RV and lifted her ticket all while her friends partied unknowingly outside.

Kelly certainly never expected to find herself at the End Zone moments before kickoff. She still doesn't quite believe she's here, but she's taking it fairly well.

"The End Zone?" she slurs to her friend (another fairly snookered young woman whose ticket to the game was swiped along with Kelly's). "I'm in the Twilight Zone right now."

Kelly's friend doesn't laugh.

Then there's Chet, who's been jawing with Kyle for a little bit. A 50ish-looking guy with working man's hands, Chet tells anyone who'll listen about how he had a pair of tickets to tonight's game but sold them, mostly out of spite. Chet's been a Patriots season-ticket holder for 14 years. He had some quality seats at the old stadium. But in the new stadium's design, his former assignment is part of the ultraexpensive club section (the one that has its own bar), so he couldn't afford to hold onto his spot. What the club offered him as an alternative were some relatively expensive seats in the upper reaches of Gillette. He took the offer, but he's not at all happy about it, making him one of a relatively small number of Patriots fans who aren't pleased with the new facility.

"I had to pay double to get worse seats," Chet grumbles. "And what did I gain? Six inches of knee room and a fuckin' cup holder."

So what did Chet do for the first-ever game in the offending new structure? He drove out to Foxborough and sold his seats—added knee room, cup holder, and all—to a couple of Steelers fans. He manages to gloat and grouse about it all in one breath. "I got 400 bucks for two tickets," he says. "I hope they choke on them."

Doug and Maura wish they'd met Chet earlier, when they were still looking for tickets. They'd have been happy to choke on Chet's.

Maura's a Pennsylvania native and a huge Steelers fan. Doug, her husband, is mostly along for the ride. They drove down from Manchester, New Hampshire, and did everything they could to find a scalper they could afford—they were willing to go $200 a pop—but only got one ticket. Maura didn't want to go into the stadium without Doug, so they resold their ticket for $300. They made $100, which isn't bad for a 15-minute investment.

Maura, a wispy blond who's retained a schoolgirl beauty into her early 30s, and tall, square-shouldered, brown-haired Doug are pleasant enough, even though they didn't really get what they wanted. And they actually seem fairly content to have tried and (sort of) failed. The way they're looking at it, at least they're drinking on someone else's dime.

Louis is a dyed-in-the-wool Pats fan, a guy my age, mid-30s, who tried to get a scalped ticket, too, but just couldn't afford it. He's unhappy about that, but he's the sort of jolly type to whom "pissed off" never really manages to stick. Besides, he's excited enough about what he sees as the start of a run to a second championship that he's unable to concentrate on his misfortune.

The guy we'll all end up calling Mr. Stats behind his back (we'll all hate him, too) wouldn't take a ticket if you offered it to him free. He's been telling anyone who'll listen about how he only came out to Foxborough to tailgate with some of his friends. He found the tailgating disappointingly tame. "The worst in the NFL," he says. Mr. Stats likes to rate things.

Surprisingly enough, no one asks Mr. Stats to rank the quality of the tailgating in the league's 31 other cities. No one's planning to do any traveling this season, I guess.

There's a grinning, drunken homophobe seated just down the bar to my left, who hisses repeatedly about how he gave up his effort to bag a scalped ticket after falling victim to a wanton, if clearly fictional, act of sexual harassment. He was pushing his way through a crowd, he says, just trying to find a scalper, when out of nowhere "some homo grabbed my ass." (It takes no particular deductive talent to determine that this is bullshit. For one thing, the guy makes it clear every time he attempts to speak that his ass might as easily have been pinched by a pink elephant as by a "homo." For another, it couldn't be more apparent that no one, gay or straight, has ever grabbed this guy's ass. Not even once. Not ever.)

I don't know what specifically has brought the assembled others here, but I do know that there are many of them, including (if a quick count of game jerseys means anything) two Antowain Smiths, a Sam Gash, a Tedy Bruschi, three Ty Laws, two Drew Bledsoes, and a single Tom Brady. There's not one Adam Vinatieri in the place.

And as far as I can tell (I don't dare ask), there are exactly four of us here who aren't expecting to see the Patriots stomp the Steelers.

Doug and Maura are certainly figuring on a Steelers win.

Mr. Stats is intent on telling anyone who'll listen that the Patriots are the 17th-best team in the NFL. They were the 17th-best team in the NFL last year, too, he says. So how does he account for the Super Bowl victory in February? Simple: "Miracles happen." He's got no data to back up his miracle theory, but then again he doesn't seem to have any actual data to back up any of his claims. He assures us his assessment of the Pats is based on statistics; he just doesn't happen to have the numbers handy. The same goes for his claim that the Steelers are the league's fourth-best team. (As with his tailgate rankings, no one thinks to ask him which teams are the top three.)

And then there's me.

It's not like I don't want the Patriots to beat the Steelers. I very much want the Pats to win. In fact, I almost always want the Pats to win (except when they play my team, the Oakland Raiders). It's just that even after their stunning Super Bowl win, I can't quite bring myself to believe in this team.

I grew up with this team, or at least it was a team with the same name as this one. I've been watching them and silently, mostly hopelessly, rooting for something wonderful to happen with them for as long as I can remember. But I've never been able to invest my deepest fan emotions in them. I couldn't bear the heartache.

I know what happened in New Orleans in February wasn't a miracle but an actual victory by an actual Super Bowl championship team, a team that earned everything it got. Still, I can't help but feel like there's something fragile, something apt to crack at any moment, about these defending champions.

Besides, I pride myself on being a realist when it comes to sizing up football games. I always root for the team I want to win, but I never fool myself into believing something will happen just because I want it to. Years of playing in office football pools and making the occasional bet on a game have taught me that while following the game is an emotional pursuit, picking winners can't be.

I figure the oddsmakers have tagged the Steelers as three-point favorites in a big away game for a reason. I figure that reason is probably their defense and maybe their running back, Jerome Bettis. And I simply have more faith in the oddsmakers and a solid running back than I do in the Pats.

I'm not here to be a jerk, though. So, unlike Mr. Stats, I have no interest in telling anyone what I think the outcome of this game will be. I'm here because I've decided it's time I figured out what makes a Patriots fan. I want to know how to believe in the home team. I want to know what keeps these people hanging on.

Tonight, it's not so hard to see what makes these fans tick. In spite of my reservations and in stark contrast to the immovable Mr. Stats' assertions, I can see how a person can believe in the Patriots. These Pats look like they quite possibly could be the best team in the NFL once again.

We don't get far into the game before it becomes clear that it's going to be a long night for the Steelers, who may or may not be the fourth-best team in the league, but are without question a damned good team.

After Pittsburgh quarterback Kordell Stewart throws his second interception of the night, even Chet stops grumbling. He's still angry at Patriots owner/Gillette Stadium builder Bob Kraft, but he's showing his fan colors more and more openly. He taunts Stewart through the TV, opining that the Steelers would be better off with backup QB Tommy Maddox under center. He laughs as ABC offers a shot of Steelers coach Bill Cowher shaking his head after his team has committed penalties on two straight plays. "Hey, Cowher," he yells, "take a bite of my ass!"

Louis spends much of the first half loudly voicing his disdain for "nonbelievers." He's comfortable enough with Maura, mostly because she's beautiful, but he makes it clear to any other non–New England fans in earshot that he's not planning to put up with us.

Though the game is still close at the end of the first half, it's clear the Patriots have the momentum. And while momentum may be an overrated intangible on the football field, it's more than enough to keep spirits high at the End Zone. The buzz of the crowd remains loud through halftime, forcing both Drew Bledsoes to take their cell phone conversations outside.

As the second half gets underway, Kelly moves into frat party mode. Every time the Patriots' offense moves the ball more than half a yard, her drink goes up over her head and her voice rings out across the bar: "Social!"

When the Pats go up 17–7 early in the third quarter, Louis bounds off his bar stool, high-fiving anyone within reach and hooting, "You nonbelievers, fuck you all!"

I try hard not to meet Louis's gaze as he scans the room. Too hard. He zeroes in on me. "Are you a nonbeliever?" he demands. "Are you a nonbeliever?" And even though I'm slowly starting to think maybe I could believe, I can't lie to the man. I'm not there yet.

"I guess I'm a nonbeliever," I offer with what I hope is enough contrition in my voice to make Louis at least feel like he's not being challenged.

"Asshole," he taunts. It's mostly good natured, but I'm inclined nonetheless to keep an eye on Louis for the rest of the night, especially since Mr. Stats, who might have served as a nifty lightning rod, has disappeared.

As the third quarter wraps up with New England ahead 27–7, Maura begins to absorb a good bit of ribbing. She takes it well, as does Doug.

The couple's halftime question about the quickest way back to New Hampshire comes back at them.

"Get on 495 South," Chet tells Doug. "When you get to the ocean, let her off."

Maura and Doug laugh because they have no choice and, I think, because they're genuinely nice people and exceedingly good sports. The rest of us laugh because we're swimming in the energy of the moment. You just can't help it.

At the two-minute warning, with the Pats up 30–7, the End Zone starts to empty out. It's quiet, but there's an energy lingering in the bar. Even the dispossessed are possessed.

Maura offers a sporting congratulations to Louis and Chet and any other Pats fans who she's offended with her presence. She and Doug head out, looking for 495 North, away from the ocean.

Kelly has disappeared, presumably off in search of that RV, and maybe some good postgame tailgating on the way there.

Chet leaves with a smile on his face, perhaps a bit less angry about a team that seems prepared to take on the world than he was at an abstract idea of a defending champion. The Pats are less the organization that took away his seats now, and more the team that brought home a Super Bowl championship.

Louis stays on until the very end of the game. I brace for what I assume is his inevitable question. I wait for him to turn to me and ask me if I'm still a nonbeliever. But the question never comes.

As soon as the game ends, Louis climbs down off his bar stool, says good-bye to Kyle and then me, and leaves.

I'm relieved. I want to be a believer now, more than I wanted to be a believer three hours earlier, but I'm still not there. And I have the feeling Louis doesn't have much use for ambivalence.

2.

Game 2 at New York Jets

Sunday, September 15, 2002

Record 1–0

There are always some things you can predict. It's true in life and it's true somewhere in the NFL on every game day.

No part of any day, outside of sunrise and sunset, is ever utterly certain, of course. But there are forever elements of certain days, and outcomes of certain games, that can only fail to surprise you. If, that is, you're paying attention.

Anyone who isn't a Las Vegas handicapper or a New York Jets fan, for example, could predict with complete confidence that the Patriots are going to thump the Jets this afternoon. Anyone who watched, or even heard about, what the Pats did to the Pittsburgh Steelers six days ago knows there's no reason to believe New England won't walk away from Giants Stadium this afternoon with its second win of the season.

It's true, the Pats are two-point underdogs according to the oddsmakers, but that's nothing more than an expression of handicapping experts' overfirm belief in home-field advantage. The formula for setting odds on NFL games starts with the home team favored by three. So the Jets were giving three points in this match as soon as the 2002 season schedule was set. Actual stats related to players and performance were factored in only after the results from week 1 were posted. The Jets opened their season with a 37–31 road victory in Buffalo, which isn't entirely unimpressive even if Buffalo has the look of a team destined to lose a lot more games than it will win this season. The Pats opened with a big home win over a team that many had tagged as one of the best in the league.

And while the actual numbers from those games only brought the line down to the Jets -2, the adjustment still means the Pats have actually come out slightly ahead in the mathematics.

John, Don, and I all know what's going to happen in this game. Indeed, our confidence in the Pats' chances today played a not-insignificant role in our decision to spend the better part of our morning driving down from Massachusetts to Manhattan.

We didn't make the journey to NYC with the hope of taunting anyone, mind you. We all have our own reasons for taking the road trip, but none of them have anything to do with a desire to act like assholes.

I've come to get a look at expatriate Patriots fans. There's a little bit of everything in New York City, and that includes a little community of Pats fans, most of them transplants from New England. And there are enough of those that I knew there would be a bar somewhere in the city that catered specifically to them. I found it, or at least I was told I'd found it, in Mo's Caribbean, a restaurant and sports bar on Manhattan's East Side. So I've come down to check the scene at Mo's, to find out what it's like when your team not only isn't the local one, but is one of the home team's most hated rivals.

Don, who is probably the most dedicated, knowledgeable, and intelligent sports fan I've ever known, is here out of a love of fan adventures. He's one of these guys who, when he travels, almost invariably includes a game in his itinerary. He simply enjoys watching sporting events in new and unfamiliar settings. He got up early this morning to make the drive down from Nashua, New Hampshire, to meet up with me in Holyoke, Massachusetts.

John, too, made an early morning drive to Holyoke to meet up for the trip to New York, coming out 90 miles from his home in Boston to do it. This isn't the first time in the 22 years we've known each other that I've talked John into accompanying me on a mostly pointless road trip. There was a time years ago when this sort of thing happened fairly regularly—a jaunt down to NYC just for a change of pace; a 3 A.M. drive to Cape Cod to drop in on friends, that sort of thing. And while those days are long gone, this trip wasn't a particularly hard sell. Even if it weren't for the old-time's-sake aspect of the day, there would have been the fact that John likes discovering a good bar as much as he likes watching the Pats. He's not a drunk or anything, just one of those guys who enjoys the social aspects of bar culture. And John is a Pats fan. He's here for the twofer.

Still, none of us would have made the trip if we didn't believe the Pats were headed for victory. It would have made no sense to journey down into enemy territory just to be taunted. And no one in sports taunts with the ferocity of Jets fans.

I hate Jets fans. I hate their team, too. But the latter sentiment only follows the former.

Jets fans embody the worst characteristics of New Yorkers. They are loud and eternally full of themselves, overconfident in their team, bad winners, and even worse losers.

There's no question but that New York is a great city, probably the best in America (though not a tenth as great as London). And so the sense of certainty some New Yorkers exude with regard to themselves and their city, while undoubtedly obnoxious, is in no way impossible to understand. But confidence unbalanced by modesty ought at the very least to be balanced by a certain degree of realism. And New Yorkers have a way of missing both, of forgetting, for instance, that the mere act of living in a world-class city doesn't make you a world-class human being. Just like the mere act of living in Boston doesn't make you an intellectual or the mere act of living in L.A. doesn't make you a movie mogul. Nor do many New Yorkers seem to understand that not everyone wishes we could live in their city. From those of us who'd rather avoid urban living altogether to those who actually prefer places like Chicago, Miami, and San Francisco, there's a nation full of people who'd really rather visit NYC than live there. We know being a New Yorker simply isn't impressive in and of itself. But try telling that to some New Yorkers.

Yankees fans are fairly difficult to take, but it has almost nothing to do with them specifically. It's just impossible not to feel slightly jealous of Yankees fans. They support a team that wins a World Series every two or three years at least. They're happy about that, which is annoying. They're confident about it, which can be endlessly vexing. And they clearly don't know how easy they have it, which is downright enraging. But they're not, as a rule, deliberately obnoxious about it.

Mets fans are a generally tolerable bunch who would be easy enough to ignore completely if it weren't for the fact that theirs was the team that benefited from Bill Buckner's failure to grasp baseball fundamentals (actually, just grasping the damned ball would have been plenty) in '86.

Giants fans are easy to get along with. They exhibit the kind of quiet confidence that comes from supporting a team that's almost always good and that wins a championship just often enough to keep the frustration from building up. (It helps that there are still Giants fans spread liberally throughout New England, people for whom rooting for the Giants is a family tradition that goes back to the time between when the Boston Braves became the Washington Redskins and the creation of the Patriots, along with the rest of the AFL, in 1960—an era when the Giants were the team that was geographically closest to New England.)

But a Jets fan, to my mind, is a New Yorker completely out of touch with reality, completely unaware that in much of the world outside of the city, people still expect each other to maintain a certain degree of decor and civility.

The Jets haven't been to a Super Bowl since '69, the year Joe Namath famously led them to an upset victory over the Baltimore Colts. In the 33 seasons since then, they've posted a winning record only nine times (including '88, when they finished 8-7-1, exactly half a game over .500). But there's still no amount of humility to be found among the team's backers. Jets fans begin each season confident that the championship to which they clearly believe their team is entitled can be no more than five months away, and they behave nastily toward fans of other teams, particularly toward fans of the Jets' nearby division rivals.

I've met a handful of civil, rational, and intelligent Jets fans in my lifetime. But I've encountered hundreds more—at games, mostly, but also in an online football forum I frequent—who have simply begged to be disliked. When their team wins, they gloat endlessly and loudly (there is no more annoying cheer in all of professional sports than "J-E-T-S, Jets, Jets, Jets," a cry always uttered with enough attitude that it comes out sounding like "Hey, fuck you"). When their team loses, they're quick to take nasty shots at fans of the opposing squad (intelligent stuff along the lines of "Yeah, well, your team still sucks"—which is more an annoyance than anything else, but fairly revealing all the same).

So I haven't come to New York to spend time with Jets fans. More than anything, I've come hoping to avoid them. But that, it turns out, isn't going to be possible.

The bartender never stops what he's doing. He doesn't even pause, really. There's too much prep work to finish. None of what he's up to needs such immediate attention that he can't answer my question—John, Don, and I are, after all, the first customers to show up at Mo's Caribbean today (we were outside waiting for the place to open at 11:30 A.M.) and the only ones in the room at the moment—but at the same time he's not about to disrupt his rhythm for me.

"Patriots fans. Dolphins fans. Jets fans," he says, dividing the room with a series of chopping hand gestures. Pats fans, it seems, get the far end of the fairly long bar. Dolphins fans have the middle. The end nearest the door belongs to Jets fans.

Each group has its own big-screen TV. They always do, the bartender says, and they will today, same as always, even though the two sets on the ends will be showing the exact same game. What's more, the bartender, who's all giant, rounded shoulders and bulging stomach—imposing in the way a mostly fat guy can be when you just know he can move fast and hit hard when he needs to—makes it seem as if there is some sort of enforced segregation in this place. No mixing of fans here.

That might be smart, I think. Might cut down on fighting.

It occurs to me that I never actually asked the bartender where we should sit. What I said was, "I'm told this is the place in New York where Patriots fans go to watch games. That true?"

The bartender, I suppose, simply jumped what he imagined was a question or two ahead of me. He got to where I was going with a minimum of small talk, which got him back to unloading the dishwasher as quickly as possible.

However indirect (and off the mark, since I never would have thought to ask any follow-up question, let alone something like

"Where do the Pats fans sit?"), the bartender's response was welcome. If he hadn't pointed out who goes where, we might easily have ended up in the middle of a pack of Miami fans. Or worse, Jets fans.

It still hasn't quite hit noon, but it's been a long drive down to Manhattan. We're all ready for a beer and a bite to eat. So we set up at the Pats end of the bar and study the taps for a moment.

Now, our helpful bartender stops and walks back toward us. He's had a thought.

"There might not be too many here today," he says. He's talking about Patriots fans. "A lot of them are at the game."

"You think so?" I reply. It's not like I hadn't expected something like that, but the disappointment in my voice is unmistakable.

"I know it," he says without a hint of apology or even sympathy. "They told me they wouldn't be here."

He starts to walk away, then glances back over his shoulder. "What did you think? Their team plays here once a season; they're gonna go to the game."

"But you'll still get some Pats fans here, right?"

"Yeah. Yeah, we'll definitely get some. But not like usual. Usually we get a lot of them. Every Sunday. It's the same guys every week. The Dolphins fans, too. That's why I know they're not gonna be here today. They come in here all the time; they tell us when they're not coming."

We order a round—two pints and a Coke; John's not ready for a real drink just yet—and talk about finding a table for lunch. Best, we figure, to get something in our stomachs and be ready to join the crowd at the bar by game time.

We get distracted, caught up in conversation about whether we shouldn't just have lunch at the bar, and suddenly we're not alone at Mo's. We're not alone on the Pats end of the bar, either. Suddenly, there are three other guys here, standing right next to us. And two of them are wearing Jets shirts.

Two of the Jets fans wear their thinning hair in mullets. The third wears a backward baseball cap and a game jersey bearing the name and number of Jets linebacker Mo Lewis. They're a bit on the loud side, too. They take a moment to jeer a guy in a Giants cap who's set up at the Jets end of the bar; he may or may not be someone they know.

We don't wait for them to spot Don's Patriots game jersey (it's got former Pats' linebacker Andy Katzenmoyer's name and number on it). We just head for the hostess station to ask for a table. We're still strangers here, after all. No reason to make any assumptions. Our best bet is to hang back a little and see what happens.

And what happens is that before too long, before our jerk-chicken sandwiches and steak fajitas ever make it to our table, the Pats side of Mo's is lousy with Jets fans. Okay, maybe there are only eight or ten of them, but that seems like a lot. What's more, besides Don there are exactly two guys here showing Patriots colors, and they don't seem all that anxious to retake their turf. They've parked themselves on the Jets end of the bar instead. Maybe they're making a point.

It's almost one o'clock, kickoff time, and I'm starting to wonder what's next—the unpredictable part of it, that is.

Even here in Manhattan, in a bar with far more Jets and Dolphins fans than Pats fans, there's a noticeably different vibe as game time approaches than what I'd seen Monday night at the End Zone. If there's a nervous energy here, it's emanating from the Dolphins fans, whose team is about to face a potent Indianapolis Colts team, and from the Jets fans.

The Pats have given no one cause to doubt them—not Don nor John nor I, nor, other than the handicappers, any NFL expert of any consequence. In fact, if anything, it appears the experts have begun to overestimate the Patriots.

ESPN.com has the Pats at the top of its weekly Power Rankings, up from sixth a week earlier.

On Wednesday, ESPN's Chris Mortensen declared both the team and its coach, Bill Belichick, the best in pro football.

"Here's what I have concluded about the Patriots: They are the best team in football," Mortensen said. "Not the Rams. Not the Steelers. Not the Eagles. Not the Raiders. Sometime during the season they became the best team, and they proved it by beating the Steelers in Pittsburgh and the Rams on the artificial turf. . . . I also have come to the conclusion that the best coach in the NFL is Bill Belichick. Does that mean the Patriots are invincible? We all know better, but for now they are the team to beat and nobody else."

On the same day, *USA Today* led its sports section with a feature on the champs, declaring them [the class of the NFL]. Monday Night Football analyst/football guru John Madden believes. The guys on HBO's *Inside the NFL* believe. Virtually everyone, everywhere concedes that the Pats are a great football team.

Except for the oddsmakers. And, as John has predicted, except for me.

"You think they're gonna win today?" John asks as I wash down my chicken sandwich with a nice, hoppy microbrew.

I've known John long enough to know he never opens with his real question. So I set him up.

"Today? Yeah, they're gonna win today. You can't not beat the Jets."

"What about the season?"

"I'm still thinking nine and seven."

"That's it?" His voice is filled with feigned incredulity.

"I don't know," I offer. "Ten and six maybe. If they win their first four, maybe they'll win twelve."

John knows full well that I'll be the last guy in New England to jump on the Patriots bandwagon. I'm more than happy to run alongside, but I've done a good job keeping my feet on the ground when it comes to this team and I'm not about to make any rash moves one game into the season.

"But today, they're gonna win?" he says. And I'm not sure whether it's to make certain I haven't changed my mind or just to bring the conversation back around.

"Today, they're gonna win," I assure him.

I really am that certain. I've looked at these two teams, sized up their strengths and weaknesses—the Jets have great receivers, but no one to throw them the ball; the Pats have a serviceable offense, one that's unlikely to break the game open but certainly won't give it away, and an incredibly tough defense that should be more than the Jets' interception-prone quarterback, Vinny Testaverde, can handle—and I've come to the conclusion that the

Pats can't lose. But I'd pretend to believe that even if I really didn't, not just because of my feelings about the Jets, but because as far as I know we're among the few here at Mo's who care about the Pats. We're outnumbered by Jets and Dolphins fans and it feels like a little wagon-circling may be in order.

There are always things that are impossible to predict. It's true throughout the NFL on every single game day. And it's true wherever you find yourself in life. Things you think you know are just forever turning out to be dead wrong.

I was wrong, for example, about there being a dearth of Patriots fans at Mo's Caribbean today. This becomes clear as soon as the Pats-Jets game really gets moving.

That doesn't happen right away, though. The game remains scoreless through the first quarter and silence reigns at both ends of the bar. If it weren't for the sight of game jerseys and team caps, you'd have a hard time confirming there was a single Pats or Jets fan in the place.

Through the early part of the afternoon, the only energy at Mo's comes from the center of the bar, where a crowd of Dolphins fans—there are about a dozen of them, all but one male, all in their mid-to-late 30s—is jubilant. Their team goes up 14–0 over Indianapolis in the first quarter. Their quarterback, Jay Fiedler, is throwing the ball almost flawlessly. And their new star, running back Ricky Williams, is proving he's worth his big free-agent contract every time he touches the ball.

Pulled along by a walking stereotype of a loud, hyperkinetic, little Italian guy, wearing a Zach Thomas game jersey and orange shorts, the Dolphins fans are shouting, stomping, and pounding on the bar. Little Zach runs back and forth between his buddies at the center of the bar and a covered pool table pushed into the back corner of the restaurant. One of the many smaller screen TVs that hang throughout Mo's is right above the table and the Dolphins-Colts game is playing there as well. Little Zach spends more time than anyone really ought to be comfortable with watching his team on that screen while making humping motions toward the pool table. He's a bit over-stimulated, it seems.

"It's hard to keep your eyes on the Patriots," John says. "There's too much going on."

He's not just kidding.

But after a rough start to the second quarter, the Pats start to come on. The defense is holding strong, keeping the Jets out of scoring position. And the offense begins to do its job, too. Not quite four minutes into the quarter, Pats running back Antowain Smith breaks open an 18-yard rush.

"Yeah! Yeah! Yeah!" I yell at the top of my lungs as Smith bullies his way down the field. Then looking around to see if the Jets fans are glaring at me, I spot another guy cheering the Pats. He's by himself, near the Jets fans at the Pats end of the bar, a big guy with a close-cropped hairdo. He's not exactly making a spectacle of himself, but neither is he trying to hide. It makes me feel a bit more secure.

The Fins fans continue to be the loudest in the place, though.

Late in the second quarter, Williams breaks open a long run and the Miami fans jump up and down in unison, shaking the entire room.

"Run, fucking Ricky, run!" Zach Thomas screams at the TV.

The Pats are winning by now, too, but it's impossible not to be distracted by the scene in the middle of the bar, where the Dolphins fans are drinking vodka shots to celebrate, it seems, every successful play.

"Happy, happy Rickeeeeee!" Zach Thomas yells as our old friend the burly bartender, unprompted, refills his glass with Absolut.

But when the Pats do well—when they score, when they recover a fumble—the cheers go up. And, glancing around the bar, I see there are covert Pats fans everywhere. They're at the Jets end of the bar. They're in the back of the room with us. And they're gathered near the big guy I spotted earlier, standing right behind the Jets fans who have taken over their territory. They get louder and louder as the game goes on, and by the middle of the third quarter, even the Dolphins fans have taken notice.

At the end of the third quarter, Pats safety Victor Green intercepts Vinny Testaverde and runs 90 yards for a touchdown. And then, something happens that I would have never predicted. Patriots and Dolphins fans, under most circumstances bitter enemies, band together to taunt the home crowd.

"J-E-T-S. Suck, suck, suck!" Zach Thomas yells it. And all of his buddies. The guys in the Pats caps on the Jets end of the bar yell it, too. And the half-dozen Pats fans now closing ranks on the Jets fan invaders at the far end of the bar.

Don yells, too. And so do I. You don't have to be on the Patriots bandwagon to appreciate a victory. You certainly don't have to believe in the Pats to hate the Jets. And knowing Jets fans, you can't feel bad about taking the chance to taunt them. They've earned it a thousand times over.

Two minutes later, the Jets score what will be their only touchdown of the game. It doesn't matter, and everyone here—including the Jets fans—knows it. The Jets are outclassed by a team that is unlikely to get short shrift from the oddsmakers—or from me—any time in the near future

Spirits are as high among Pats fans now as they ever were with the Dolphins crowd. A minute and a half into the fourth quarter, as the Pats offense moves the ball down the field systematically, I turn to Don and say, "This is great. Lets the defense get some rest."

"Yeah," he laughs, "'cause it really wears you out running back all those interceptions for touchdowns."

Late in the game, as backup quarterback Damon Huard leads the Pats who have sealed a victory, we focus on the Dolphins-Colts game once again.

The Colts are driving to tie the score, a last-chance effort that finally fails. It's a disappointing outcome from a Pats fan's perspective. It's always better when a division rival drops a game. But it's hard not to feel happy for the Fins fans, who were with us when it counted.

As the Patriots game winds down, and the Pats' second team moves toward a final touchdown that will put the icing on the Jets' embarrassment, a big, 35ish-looking guy in a black T-shirt wanders into Mo's and walks up to Don.

"You guys Pats fans?"

"We are," Don tells him.

He says he's just come from another bar where, in spite of what's happened in this game, he's been harassed mercilessly by a roomful of Jets fans. No kidding, I think, Jets fans who don't know when to shut up. Shocking.

Kevin Faulk goes into the end zone on an easy two-yard run. The score is 44–7.

"This is so satisfying," the new guy says. "This is like a filet mignon from Peter Lugar's."

I've never been. Not much for steak houses, even the legendary variety. But the analogy makes sense. There are few things in life quite as deliciously unpredictable as losing a side of a bar that was never yours to begin with only to win it back.

I watch the Jets who parked in Patriots territory early in the day pay their tab and begin the long walk across the room to the door. And I think about how it's going to be a really short drive home.

3.

Game 3 vs. Kansas City Chiefs

Sunday, September 22, 2002
Record 2–0

I don't want to be a black cat. I don't want to be a broken mirror. Or a hat on the bed.

I suppose that really ought to go without saying. No one ever wants to be a source of bad fortune. But that's really not what I mean.

I know I'm not really anyone's bad luck charm. I couldn't be. Because there's no such thing as a jinx. No person has the power to affect events in which he's not an active participant simply by being witness to them. And every rational person in the world knows that.

The trouble is, sports fans, particularly sports fans caught up in the emotional experience of a close game, aren't exactly the world's most rational people. Fans, in fact, can be every bit as neurotically fixed on the odd elements of behavior and happenstance that they believe bring on good and bad fortune as are the athletes on the field.

For every slugger who refuses to shave during a hitting streak there are untold numbers of fans who believe that same streak will end if they fail to take three quick sips of beer every time the player steps up to bat. For every wide receiver who believes the socks he wears during a game determine whether he catches a touchdown pass, there are fans who believe the end of the couch they sit on is the real key to whether that same touchdown happens. For every team whose members believe their pregame ritual, properly performed, can ward off evil and mischievous spirits, there are fans who believe their actions, the actions of others, and in some case the very presence of the wrong person, can cost their team a game.

And the fear of jinxes is every bit as real as the actual existence of jinxes isn't.

I know this, because I've felt that fear. I've been through the mental processes that allow thoughts about jinxes to take hold, to take over, even while the rational mind cries out to be heard. I've been in the position of becoming agitated at the presence of a perceived source of bad luck even while deep within I knew I was behaving like a madman. I've experienced the inability to stop myself from engaging in the kind of narcissistic, delusional thinking toward which I can be nothing short of disdainful in calmer, less charged moments.

There have been more times in my life than I'd like to admit, for instance, when I've come within immeasurably tiny distances of believing, actually *believing*, that any time my wife walked into the living room while I was watching a game, something bad was bound to happen to my team.

Now, I love my wife. And I feel fairly bad about abandoning her on Sundays five months a year (the woman simply can't abide football). So, for the most part, I actually like to see her walk into the room when I'm watching a game. And, as noted, I do my best to avoid engaging in the kind of magical thinking that leads a person to believe something happening in his living room could possibly affect the outcome of a football game taking place as much as a continent away. But it happens just the same.

The Raiders (or the Pats; or, you know, whatever team I happen to have money riding on) set up on their opponents' goal line trailing by four points with two and a half minutes left to play. I'm on the edge of the couch, elbows on my knees, hands in my hair, trying hard not to breathe in the wrong direction. Then my wife steps in, blissfully unaware of the fact that she's bringing bad luck to my team, blissfully unaware, for that matter, that my team is even in need of a blessing. "How's it going out here?" she'll ask innocently, just trying to be friendly. "Fine," I'll snap back. "It's going just fine." The tone of my voice will make it clear that what I really mean is, "Please, please go away. You're messing things up." She'll leave the room, knowing only that it must be the game, not her, that has put me in a bad mood. I'll watch her go, simultaneously feeling bad for letting my absurd anxieties ruin a chance check-in with her and bracing for the turnover I know is now inevitable.

So I know there's no breaking yourself out of the jinx-fear mind-set once it's taken hold. And I know, consequently, that whether jinxes do or don't exist isn't really the question before me this afternoon. Neither is whether I am, in fact, a jinx. What's important right now is whether the guys I'm sitting with in Gillette Stadium, the guys who have been kind enough to include me in their intense, full day of tailgating and game watching, believe I'm a jinx.

At the moment, it seems at least one of them does.

"You know if they lose, you can never come to another game, right?" Dave tells me. There's enough of a tone of levity in his voice to let me know he's only kidding, even though I don't really know Dave at all. But I'm not particularly concerned about what Dave thinks at the moment. I'm concerned about what Dave will think as the game moves on.

It's the very beginning of the second quarter and the Kansas City Chiefs have just scored their first touchdown of the day on a 14-yard pass from Trent Green to Eddie Kennison. The Chiefs are now up 10–0 in a game where the Pats have shown almost nothing on offense.

The defending champion Pats, who have been almost universally anointed the "best team in football" as a result of their big wins against the Steelers and Jets, seem to be specializing this afternoon in penalties and dropped passes. The Chiefs, meanwhile, look like they're beginning to get into a groove.

It appears the day may go badly for New England. That hasn't happened in quite some time. The Patriots last lost a game on November 18, 2001. They've won 11 matches since then, including a Super Bowl. And as Dave looks around trying to see what's different, the first thing his eyes fall on is me.

Dave doesn't really know me. We met just before seven this morning at his home in Smithfield, Rhode Island. Shannon and Billy, the other guys we're sitting with, on the other hand, have been coming to Patriots games with Dave for years. If Dave ever had any reason to suspect either of his old friends might be jinxes, it's clearly been erased by the team's last five home games.

The new stadium, too, has been tested for jinx potential and come up clean. And while there are certainly plenty of things that make today different from the days on which the Pats' last five games in Foxborough were played—weather more like one would expect in late August than in late September, for example, or, say, an additional 8,000 fans in the stands (any one of whom might easily be a Schleprock)—sports fan jinx investigations typically proceed from the expectation that the culprit must be close at hand.

And since I'm the only wild card in sight, it stands to unreason that I have to be the evil force behind the Pats' shoddy play.

I chuckle in response to Dave's warning, but there's concern hidden not very deep beneath my chuckle. I have no way of knowing whether Shannon and Billy also have the idea that I've brought bad fortune to the Patriots. And even if they don't think I'm trouble now, I can't even begin to guess what they might come to believe if things keep going badly for their team.

There's no question in my mind but that these are nice guys. But irrationality doesn't know from nice. So all I can think about is how I came into Foxborough with these guys—on their bus. What if the Pats lose and I end up getting ditched at the stadium?

My experience with oddball fan behavior notwithstanding, I'm aware that my worries are probably as silly as Dave's idea that I'm a jinx. I've been hanging out with Dave, Shannon, Billy, and a bunch of their buddies all day long and not one of them has proven to be anything but friendly and welcoming. Indeed, they've been even more open and accepting of my presence than I'd hoped.

I found Shannon through David, a family friend. Shannon's a health teacher at Milford High School, where David is the physical education/health director. When David heard I was looking to hook up with some dedicated Pats fans, he thought immediately of Shannon. He knew that Shannon and his pals were diehards. He also knew they took their tailgating extremely seriously. He knew, in short, that Shannon was precisely the type of fan I was looking to meet.

I talked to Shannon. He talked to his friends. And they found a game, this one, to which they had a spare ticket. We made arrangements to get together.

It became clear to me just how dedicated Shannon and his pals are to the Pats when I left Northampton at 4:45 A.M., en route to meet Shannon.

I met Shannon, a Worcester resident, in the central Massachusetts town of Sutton at 6. From there, we drove to Dave's house in North Smithfield, just over the border from Massachusetts. That's where we met up with the others. That's where they keep the bus.

The bus is a new part of the package. The guys—Shannon, Dave, Billy, Ricky, Keith, Mike, and Pep—picked it up earlier in the year to replace the van they'd been driving to Pats games for the past several years.

They bought a used Harvard University shuttle bus, painted a Patriots logo on the driver's side, slapped some Pats stickers on the windows, and rigged the thing as an impressive tailgating headquarters. There's a satellite TV hookup. There's a canopy that attaches to the back of the bus, providing shade and cover for the guys and reducing glare on the big-screen TV they station in an open rear window. There's storage space for a gasoline-fueled generator, a pair of liquid propane grills, lawn chairs, coolers, and whatever else the guys might deem necessary. All that's missing is a refrigerator and a bathroom.

Just seeing a thing like the game bus sitting in a driveway is a little overwhelming.

You take a look at that bus sitting there and you think, these guys aren't just regular old fans. They're not even just regular old season-ticket holders. These guys have made a long-term investment in their team. Oh, for God's sake, what you think is precisely this: "Holy shit. These guys bought a bus—*a bus*—just to take to football games."

It's more than a little overwhelming to arrive in Foxborough on that bus just after 8 A.M. only to find yourself sitting in a quickly lengthening line of cars, buses, vans, and RVs waiting for a parking lot (a field, really) across Route 1 from the stadium to open up.

As we stood outside the bus stretching our legs, an attendant worked the line, collecting parking fees in advance from as many vehicles as possible. The point wasn't to get the money in hand, but to ensure things would go as smoothly as possible once they began letting traffic move into the lot.

Guys anxious to get their parties started left vehicles in the hands of their unfortunate drivers and walked just beyond the boundary ropes and onto the field. There, they cracked open beers and, in a weirdly balletic display, maneuvered through a series of overlapping, sometimes interwoven games of catch.

Deeper into the lot, guys in lawn chairs set up camp in what they were determined to make certain would become their parking spaces. "Jesus," I thought. "They must love those goddamned spots."

At 8:30, the lot attendants removed the ropes blocking the entrance to the field and the rush was on. I jumped onto the bus just as Billy started to pull away, stumbled into the nearest open seat, and held on with all my strength as we rocketed across that field like some kind of stadium-side homesteaders.

We pulled into the guys' usual spot and disembarked. And then the fellas swung into action, moving fluidly in patterns established over a long evolutionary period (though newly adapted from van to bus), setting up for a day of tailgating in less time than it would take most fans to fix a halftime snack.

By nine o'clock, a tent was up; the satellite dish was aimed; the generator was running; ESPN was on the TV; beers were opened; off to the side, a game of pitch was under way; and Mike, the cook of the bunch, had what looked to be about five pounds of bacon frying on the gas grills.

The next three and a half hours passed in a blur of endlessly active nothingness.

There was a breakfast of scrambled eggs, hash browns, and bacon, followed almost immediately, it seemed, by a lunch of barbecued ribs. (Later, after the game, there would be pulled-pork sandwiches, corn on the cob, and grilled potatoes. We'd never quite make it to the teriyaki steak.)

There were a whole lot of guys in their early 30s who had known each other since they were kids interacting as fluidly as such long-time friends will in a familiar setting, trading unfathomable inside jokes, half-told vacation stories, and less-than-half-told memories, all rendered in the unmistakable accent of the Massachusetts–Rhode Island border region where the guys grew up.

There was a good deal of boys being boys, of telling the stranger (better still, the journalist stranger) every embarrassing story about the other guys they could summon. There was horseplay, raised voices, and mock threats. There were the fart jokes. And, of course, there was the odd sexual posturing, the "my cock is so big" comments, that invariably colors the play of men among men. There was even some football talk—though not nearly as much as I would have expected—most of it centered on the assumption that the Patriots were about to waltz to a victory over the Chiefs and a 3–0 start to their postchampionship season.

Then came the game.

The guys don't all have seats together (in fact, they don't all have seats), so we split up as we head out across the street to Gillette. Mike and Pep head in together. Ricky and Keith stay on at the bus, where they'll watch the game on satellite. Shannon, Dave, Billy, and I head toward seats in section 236, off to the shady side of the end zone nearest Route 1.

Gillette is every bit the impressive place it's been described as. Except for the fact that there aren't enough restrooms, it's damned near perfect. Where Foxboro Stadium was cramped and closed, Gillette is big and wide open. We enter into an expansive concourse that offers a full view of the field from the Route 1 side end zone and gives way to wide passages lined with all variety of concessions (overpriced, of course; this is an NFL game, after all). The stairway to our section is clearly marked, as are the rows. And the seats, while hardly of the first-class section variety, are damned roomy by sports venue standards.

I dawdle a bit, taking it all in, and Shannon hangs back to make sure I don't get lost. Tall and shaven-headed with a wide smile forever plastered across his narrow face, Shannon comes off as the model of a gentle giant. He's clearly the kind of guy who was made to teach kids. His instinct is to keep an eye out for those who have put their trust in him.

Even with my curiosity slowing us down, we beat big-bellied but tough-looking Billy and solid, conservatively kept Dave to our seats; they're off picking up a round of expensive draft beers.

We're all together again for less than five minutes before the opening kickoff. And things start off ugly.

With the Pats' slow, clumsy start, the side of Patriots' fandom I've known all my life starts to emerge. The guys get frustrated. They begin to believe there's some kind of universal plot to derail their team. And they look around for something, someone, to blame for the Pats' sudden reversal of fortune.

Three penalties on the Pats early in the game—two on the defense during Kansas City's first drive, one on the punt-return team—and Shannon believes the officials are gunning for his team.

Dave watches Troy Brown drop what should have been an easy pass, shakes his head, and offers, "Things to come here today, boys." Moments later, after the punting team commits yet another penalty to negate a great stop, Dave mutters, "They can't go 3–0. They can't go 3–0." Not a single point has been scored by either team.

The guys sitting in front of us conclude that Tom Brady's reported relationship with Tara Reid, a young actress of little note, is bringing about the bad mojo.

And then, after that Green-to-Kennison touchdown, Dave concludes that it's me.

Eight tense minutes pass before Kevin Faulk catches a 23-yard touchdown pass to get the Pats on the board. For reasons that defy both logic and divination, the team tries a two-point conversion after the score. They miss it, and I try my best to look at my shoes. But I can't help but join the debate over whether the attempt made sense; my conservative outlook on football strategy holds that you never go for two unless you have to. Dave agrees with me. Shannon and Billy are willing to trust Bill Belichick's decision making. I'm just as happy to be on Dave's side.

Seconds before halftime, Adam Vinatieri adds a 37-yard field goal to bring the Pats within a point (that wasted point-after try accounts for the difference) and things start to feel a lot more relaxed.

Priest Holmes and Trent Green conspire to put me back in the hot seat early in the third quarter, with a three-yard touchdown pass. But Troy Brown brings it back around the Patriots' way midway through the period with a nine-yard catch for a score. This time, the two-point try is good and the Pats make it even.

The Pats end the third quarter driving and begin the fourth with a touchdown pass from Brady to tight end Daniel Graham. A minute and a half later, the Pats capitalize on a Kansas City fumble to score again, this time on a long pass to David Patten. They're up 14.

I'm feeling fairly confident that I won't be having to answer for jinxing the team after all. That's good all by itself. And then things get even better—for me.

Billy pulls out his betting card to have a look. And, peeking at the card over Billy's shoulder, Dave discovers that his buddy is a traitor to the cause. Billy's got the Chiefs. Not a bad bet, all in all. Kansas City's getting eight and a half points today. That's a big spread in any NFL game, and way more points than any team ought to be giving to the Chiefs and their explosive offense.

The way Dave sees things, though, Billy has betrayed the Pats. "You picked who?" Dave demands of Billy. "You picked who?" He seizes Billy's card and tears it up.

Now I feel completely comfortable. I'm no longer worried about losing my ride (and quite sure I never needed to be in the first place). I'm also no longer worried about being branded a jinx.

Anything bad that goes down from here on out will be Billy's responsibility, not mine.

How do I know? Because I've been down this road before, too. An investigation into a football team's turn of bad luck will always start with a look at what's different. But the discovery of a betrayal close to home invariably obviates all other lines of inquiry.

This new sense of security allows me to voice the concern that has come over me as I've watched the Pats' offense struggle and, more to the point, as I've watched Holmes run all over the Patriots' D. I'm worried about the fact that the Pats are about to play two road games against the San Diego Chargers and Miami Dolphins, teams that certainly have better defenses and arguably better running backs than the Chiefs.

Dave doesn't buy into my fears.

"San Diego's defense is overrated," he says. (A few hours later, after San Diego's defense posts a safety, a touchdown, two interceptions, and three sacks against Arizona, I'll wonder whether Dave's point of view has changed.) I begin to formulate an argument to the contrary, but the game isn't quite over and there's no telling what's still to come (Billy's betrayal or none) so I decide it's best to keep it to myself.

Turns out it's a good decision. After the teams trade touchdowns in the middle of the fourth quarter, Holmes logs two late-rushing touchdowns, the second of them coming as time expires in regulation play, and ties the game.

And now, as the teams head into overtime, Billy is truly on the hook.

"This is your fault," Dave tells him as the captains trot out onto the field for the coin toss.

There's been virtually no defense for the last quarter of the game. So it looks like whichever team begins OT with the ball is bound to win the game. If ever the Pats needed a jinx-free moment it's now.

The Chiefs are the visiting team, so they get to call the toss.

They call heads.

It comes up tails.

The Pats take the kickoff and spend the better part of five minutes of game time driving down the field. At 4:40, Vinatieri puts up a 35-yard field goal. And the Patriots escape the day with a win.

They can, it seems, go 3–0. Better still, it appears both Billy and I are in the clear.

The question that occurs to me as I walk across Route 1 on my way back to the bus is, can the Pats go 4–0? We've lost Dave and Billy in the crowd. So it's just me and Shannon, who hasn't had much to say all afternoon. But I figure he's the kind of guy who gets too caught up in watching a game to be social. He's been friendly otherwise. So as we cut through a patch of woods on our way back to the parking lot and the bus, I ask him what he thinks about the weeks ahead.

He doesn't have much to say on the matter, except to acknowledge he's a bit concerned. He moves quickly to change the subject, telling me a story about the time some guys tried to find a shorter shortcut through these woods and ended up getting lost.

I get the message. Shannon doesn't want to talk about San Diego. Or Miami. I think maybe he's worried that the mere act of talking about the Pats' upcoming games will bring on bad luck.

Me, I'm a little tired and a lot sunburned. I'm also glad to have had the chance to spend the day with Shannon and his buddies. So while I'm actually more than a little concerned about what's next for the Patriots, I decide once again that it's probably best to keep my thoughts to myself.

4.

Game 4 at San Diego Chargers

Sunday, September 29, 2002
Record 3–0

I'm almost afraid to tell John the truth about where my pro football loyalties lie. But I'm not about to lie to the guy.

"You said you're a big football fan, but you're not really a Patriots fan," John says, setting up the question I'd been hoping he wouldn't ask. "Are you just a football fan, not a fan of any team?"

Shit, I think. *Oh, fucking shit.*

Now I've gotta let the damned cat out of the bag. And that's no minor matter. I'm about to tell John that I'm an Oakland Raiders fan. I'm about to reveal this bit of information to a guy who may be the most intense New England Patriots fan on the planet, a hard-line homer who's already told me he doesn't care for New Englanders who aren't loyal to the local squad and whom I've heard taunting some Miami Dolphins fan friends mercilessly.

I've been hanging out with John at his home in Warwick, Rhode Island, for less than 45 minutes, but I already know what he thinks of the Raiders and their fans. Not much, is what it boils down to. And that's hardly a surprise.

I've lived among Pats fans all my life. I'm well aware that there are very few teams Pats fans dislike more than the Raiders.

If you care about the Patriots in any way, you're almost obliged to harbor a fierce hatred for the Miami Dolphins. The Fins are not simply division rivals. Over the years, they've been one of the most consistently strong teams in the AFC East, which means they're the team that has most often stood in the way of the Pats achieving greatness (or at least transcending outright mediocrity).

And, of course, there's the Jets, a team you really can't help but loathe.

New England fans don't automatically hate the Chicago Bears, regardless of what they did to the Pats in Super Bowl XX. Nor do Pats fans feel any particular animus toward the Green Bay Packers, who made fools of New England in Super Bowl XXXI.

After the Fins and the Jets, the Raiders are the team Pats fans most despise. And, sure, Oakland is the most widely reviled team in the league, but the fact is that Pats fans have their own particular reasons for hating the silver and black.

Some of those reasons are understandable, though even those reveal a sort of regional Irish memory. Take Art Tatum's career-ending hit on Darryl Stingley in '77, which remains unforgotten and unforgiven by New England fans. Or consider the obscenely bad roughing the passer call referee Ben Dreith made against Pats defensive lineman Ray "Sugar Bear" Hamilton in '76. That call effectively knocked the Patriots out of the play-offs in a year when they seemed destined to win the Super Bowl. And while more than a quarter-century has passed, Dreith's name remains almost as widely cursed in New England as Bill Buckner's. The Raiders share the blame and the disdain purely because they were on the other side of the ball.

Another reason for Pats fans' Raider hating is substantially less understandable. That's Jim Plunkett. Long-time fans consider it some kind of affront that the Raiders were able to turn Jim Plunkett, a loser in New England, into a Super Bowl champion. (This is connected to an odd type of jealousy that crops up whenever an athlete leaves a Boston team and finds success elsewhere. It's not a condition specific to New England, of course. Sports fans everywhere hate seeing their teams' failures thrive elsewhere. It's as if there were some special kind of betrayal in it—as if an athlete deliberately held back in one town just so he could have his greatest years elsewhere.)

And at least one of the reasons Pats fans hate the Raiders, the newest of them, is patently absurd. Embarrassing, really. It's the resentment that comes from understanding on some unconscious level that the Raiders actually beat the Pats in their 2001 divisional play-off contest. The infamous "tuck rule" call that turned Tom Brady's fumble in that game into an incomplete pass, allowing New England to keep the ball and tie (then win) the game, was every bit as bad as the call against Sugar Bear Hamilton 25 years earlier.

The Raiders were winning that match, the last game ever played in Foxboro Stadium. They'd battled their way through near-blizzard conditions to lead 13–10 with less than two minutes on the clock.

Then, as the Patriots drove down the field in a last attempt to win or tie the game, Raiders' cornerback Charles Woodson charged into the Pats' backfield on a blitz, hit Brady, and knocked the ball loose. Linebacker Greg Biekert recovered for Oakland. And the game should have ended there. The Raiders should have come out onto the snow-covered field, burned up what time was left on the clock, and then headed off to Pittsburgh for the AFC championship.

What happened instead was that the officials reviewed the call on the field through instant replay and decided Brady had aborted an attempt to pass and was in the process of tucking the ball away when Woodson hit him. By rule, that tucking motion is considered part of the pass motion. And that meant the outcome of the play was not a fumble, but an incomplete forward pass. The Pats got the ball back. Adam Vinatieri hit a seemingly impossible 45-yard field goal to tie the game. Then he hit another one in overtime for the win.

Trouble is, Brady was never going to pass the ball. He pump-faked, yeah, but a pump fake isn't an attempt to pass; it's a fake. There was no tuck. The call on the field should have stood. The Raiders were robbed. And every person who saw that game and who isn't a true blue Patriots fan (or a dedicated Raider hater) knows it.

Of course, the fact that the Pats were helped along on the road to Super Bowl XXXVI doesn't render their win one bit less spectacular. But it remains the case that New England probably wouldn't have made it to the championship without a bad call going its way. And, for true believers, that's not an easy thing to live with.

I already know what John thinks about the tuck call. He announced his position on the matter soon after he welcomed me into his home.

We were watching the Dolphins–Kansas City Chiefs one o'clock game when we caught a network tease for the Raiders–Tennessee Titans matchup on tap for four (the local affiliate would be showing the Patriots–San Diego Chargers game then). And the mere mention of the Raiders was enough to elicit a derisive comment from my host.

"Hah," John scoffed. "They're still crying out there about the tuck rule and all that."

Just like that. Out of nowhere.

Well, it didn't really come out of nowhere. John wasn't actually talking to me when he made the comment. He was continuing an ongoing conversation with his TV. All football fans interact with the announcers (or imagine we do). And John is hardly the only person who's ever forgotten to leave off such conversations in the presence of other actual humans.

The last thing I want is to tell John I'm a Raiders fan only to end up in yet another debate about that stinking call. I've had my fill of those. The call was wrong. I've watched the replay 1,000 times and every single time, from every available angle, it is obvious Brady was never going to throw the ball. It was a goddamned fumble. I've tried, every time it's come up, to point out the other inarguable truth: Bad calls happen and you have to live with them. The fact that the Pats should have lost to the Raiders doesn't mean they don't deserve their Vince Lombardi trophy. But that's never been enough for Pats fans. They need you to say the call was good. And I can't do that.

So I brace a bit as I speak the words: "Actually, I'm a Raiders fan."

And because I've had a good 25 years of practice at this, I move fluidly to my next statement, leaving no space between revealing my loyalties and explaining them.

"I mean, I've never rooted against the Pats," I tell John. "I always want them to win. But I could never take it, you know? I needed to have a team that I could count on."

"Oh, yeah," he says, smiling, "I know what you're saying."

I'm more than a bit surprised. This, after all, has come from a guy I've just heard harassing one of his Dolphin fan friends over the phone (and through an answering machine). "Oh, you won't even pick up the phone?" he teased. "What, are you still crying? Hey, if your Dolphins are playing like this against Kansas City, how do you think they're gonna do against a real defense?"

So his response to my explanation about the Raiders is a pleasant surprise.

Of course, I'm not entirely certain I've heard all John has to say about Oakland. The Raiders are getting ready to face a powerful Titans team. And while I'm confident my guys will win, the fact remains that anything can happen in the NFL. And I have little doubt John, the kind of person who adopts an almost instant familiarity with you, won't hesitate to give me the same kind of razzing he's hit those Fins fans with if it works out that the Patriots have an easy day and the Raiders tank.

Perhaps even worse, I think, what if the opposite happens? What if constant updates from around the league show the Raiders rolling while we watch the Pats take a beating? That seems the path this afternoon is more likely to take, frankly. The concerns about the Pats' inability to stop the run that came over me while watching the Chiefs game haven't faded any over the last week. The Chargers, like the Pats, come into today undefeated. They've been winning mostly thanks to the success of their remarkable running back, LaDainian Tomlinson. And while I recognize that my traditional pessimism toward the Pats is probably affecting my outlook, I'm semiconvinced that New England is on the verge of a loss at San Diego.

I've only known John while things have been going his way. Watching the Dolphins lose, he's been full of energy, smiling wide, jumping around his living room, happily shouting taunts at the Dolphins through his big-screen TV.

That's exactly what I do when I'm watching a game at home and things are going my way.

What I do when things aren't going my way is a good bit uglier. I swear at the set, fume, pout, and stomp around. I don't know if John is like me in that way, too, but I'm afraid I'm going to find out.

So I still secretly cross my toes for a big Raiders win. I think maybe I should find something else to cross for the Patriots, but

I'm not entirely sure it would do any good. Besides, I need my fingers free for beer and chicken wings and my legs free for the jumping-up-and-down part of watching football. So I leave the Pats to find their own luck.

And what the hell, I think. Maybe John should keep something crossed for New England. He's the Pats fan here.

The fact that John still loves and supports the Patriots is something worth noting in itself. If I were him, I'd have jumped over to the Giants by now.

You see, John took a great big kick in the nuts from his favorite team this season.

John was a Patriots season-ticket holder from 1982 until a couple of weeks before the start of the 2002 season. That's when the team yanked his seats out from under him as a punishment for selling his tickets for one of this season's eight home games on eBay. And while the Patriots organization had every right to revoke John's status as a season-ticket holder—there are clearly stated rules prohibiting resale of tickets—I still have to wonder why they would risk alienating someone like John.

Over the course of 20 seasons, including more than a couple that the Patriots finished with fewer than a handful of wins, John missed two Pats home games. That's a game a decade.

John was there in the dreary, cramped cattle pen that was Foxboro Stadium in the rain, snow, and freezing cold, often for games that were only important in determining how high up in the draft order the Pats would pick the following spring. He was there in years when the team was lucky if it drew 20,000 fans to many games. He was there to cheer on a 1992 team quarterbacked by Hugh Millen that finished 2–14. And that was an improvement over what he'd seen in 1990, when the team finished 1–15 and never posted a single win at home.

Still, visiting John's home, a nice modern colonial in a newish-looking subdivision not far from TF Green Airport, you'd almost conclude the Pats must rank among the league's more storied franchises.

John's home office is a shrine to the Patriots with autographed photos and footballs, a Super Bowl XXXI ticket cast in Lucite, a wealth of memorabilia, all carefully displayed on a wall of shelves. A large magnet he had made for his truck reads "blue thunder, white lightning," a reference to the Pats' defense and offense. He believes it's important that he wear some kind of Pats gear every game day. He doesn't really believe that what he wears brings the team luck, but he's not taking any chances.

When John talks about how excited he was that he'd managed to score better seats for this season, moving to the 34th row on the 50 yard line, his glee is overwhelming. And when he tells me how he never got to sit in those seats, his heartache and his anger are unmistakable.

John doesn't deny he tried to sell a pair of tickets at a premium. Why bother? He was caught in the act. But he swears his motive for putting the seats up for auction was largely innocent.

When John realized he was going to have to miss his third-ever game October 13 because it fell during an anniversary trip he'd promised to take with his wife, he decided to sell his tickets for that game on eBay. He figured if he was going to miss the game, he might as well get a little something out of it. And why not? People do it all the time. Many do it strictly for profit. You can buy tickets to pretty much any sporting event you can imagine on eBay. You certainly have more than enough opportunities to pick up Pats tickets there.

Trouble is, it's against the rules to resell tickets to Patriots games. Says so right on the back of the tickets. And when the Patriots discovered that John was breaking the resale ban, they revoked his season tickets. Just stripped them away.

There was no call to say, "Hey, you can't do that." No letter asking him to cut it out. Just official legal notice that he'd lost his tickets and a check refunding the purchase price.

John believes the Patriots organization failed to recognize a critical difference between the letter and the intent of their resale rules when they yanked his tickets. As a veteran police officer—these days John works out of the Rhode Island Attorney General's Office, administering gang prevention programs for kids, but he spent years in uniform—John says he knows how to separate justice from the law.

"If I see you running a red light and I pull you over and you're on the way to the hospital, you're hurt or you're sick, I'm probably not gonna write a ticket," John says. "Technically, you broke the law, so I'm right to write a ticket, but if I did, did I do justice? No."

John doesn't think possession of a spare pair of football tickets adds up to a medical emergency, of course. But neither is auctioning tickets the same as running red lights. Mitigating circumstances are mitigating circumstances.

It's neither here nor there, however. John's attempts to regain his seats, through a meeting with team officials and, more recently, through the courts, have so far proven fruitless.

John's still trying. But for now, after 20 years as a season-ticket holder, John has been turning to eBay himself to buy tickets for the team's home games, buying from people who are wise enough to the rules to sell through third parties. When that fails, he knows he can get tickets from authorized ticket resellers (the ones people refer to as legal scalpers). The team allows those agencies to resell tickets at prices higher than face value. (No one will say why teams allow those agencies to resell tickets, but for anyone with the slightest idea of what it is that drives professional sports organizations, it isn't all that hard to guess.) John's purchased tickets to both games at Gillette Stadium so far this season—paying about $250 for a pair of tickets with face values of $75 each—and he says he plans to continue getting into games that way, because he continues to love the team even though he's not so fond of the organization.

It occurs to me that the Patriots of 10 years ago, poorly run as they may have been, might have handled John's situation more reasonably. Without a 50,000-deep waiting list for season tickets, that Patriots organization might actually have contacted John and told him what he was doing was against the rules. It might have recognized the value of a guy who's been showing up for games through thick and thin for two decades.

The current Patriots organization doesn't need to reward loyalty, and so, apparently, it isn't going to. Winning a Super Bowl changes pretty much everything, it seems. Even a few things it probably shouldn't.

As dusk drops down over Warwick, the southern California sun looks to be shining on the Pats. New England wins the coin toss and takes their opening drive 67 yards down the field to score on a five-yard Brady toss to tight end Christian Fauria.

When Fauria pulls in the touchdown, John rockets to his feet and lunges at the TV pumping his right fist.

"Yeah!"

He turns, beaming toward me.

"Yeah!"

I'm excited, too, so I offer a "Yeah," right back, though I remain seated.

Then John comes back to the couch where we've both been sitting. He extends his hand to shake. I reciprocate, of course.

A quick double pump and we both turn our eyes back to the TV. Adam Vinatieri nails the extra point. And I start to think I really do have too little faith in the Patriots.

It starts to look even better right after that. But then things begin to get frustrating.

Ronney Jenkins fumbles the post-touchdown kickoff at the Chargers' 26 yard line and the Patriots recover. But the Chargers challenge the ruling, saying Jenkins was down before the ball came out.

John isn't buying it. "I don't think so," he shouts at the TV. "It looks like fourteen-nothing to me."

The refs aren't so sure. They give the ball back to the Chargers.

"Screw you!" John shouts in disgust as the replay official announces the decision.

Four plays later, John's back in good spirits. Chargers fullback Fred McCrary puts the ball on the ground at the San Diego 39 yard line and the Pats fall on it again. This time it's clearly not going the other way.

"Try overturning that," John dares Chargers coach Marty Schottenheimer.

Schottenheimer takes the bait and loses the challenge and, by rule, a time out.

"Now here it comes," John predicts once again. "Fourteen-nothing. It's all over."

But it isn't all over. The Pats pick up just 3 yards on three plays, then opt to punt rather than attempt a 53-yard field goal.

The Chargers start out at their 13 yard line. They hand off to Tomlinson on four straight downs, netting 35 yards in the process. Then, having sucked the Patriots defensive secondary in, they call a pass play. Quarterback Drew Brees and wide receiver Curtis Conway combine for 52 yards and a touchdown. A quick Steve Christie point-after and the game is tied.

The second quarter works much the same way. The Pats start out strong, scoring on an odd Brady pass to linebacker Mike Vrabel, who lines up at tight end. Then they die down.

Vinatieri misses a 41-yard field goal attempt midquarter. Then the Chargers mount another odd scoring drive. They move the ball just 32 yards in eight plays, only to have Tomlinson break open a 37-yard touchdown run.

The game is tied heading into halftime, which isn't terrible. A tie remains anybody's game. And there's little question but that this game could go either way.

"The second half's gonna be all Patriots," John assures me.

"You think?"

"It has to be," he says. And I'm not sure whether to read his tone as one of cautious hope or stoic certainty until he gives me another clue. "You know," he says, pausing. "I'm just not impressed with San Diego." Okay, then. Hopefulness it is.

The Chargers come into the second half looking a lot more impressive. They open with a two-play drive that ends with a 58-yard touchdown run by Tomlinson. And now they're ahead 21–14.

The Patriots, meanwhile, turn far less impressive. Their first drive ends when Chargers cornerback Ryan McNeil intercepts a Brady pass at the San Diego 12 yard line.

The Chargers, plenty happy to be up by seven, run Tomlinson on play after play. Five minutes into the third quarter, Schottenheimer opts to go for it on fourth and short at his team's own 37 yard line, a gamble that could end up putting the Patriots back in the game.

"Here it comes. Here it comes," John says, inching up to the edge of his seat, ready to celebrate if the Pats D stops the conversion. But Tomlinson gets three yards and the Chargers keep the ball.

I watch the energy begin to drain out of John as he settles back onto the couch. With a full 25 minutes of game time left, this match is anything but over. And still, sometimes you can just feel that a game isn't going your team's way. Sometimes 21–14 might as well be 31–7, the score by which my wonderful, unstoppable Raiders lead their game at halftime.

I'm afraid to celebrate as I see the Raiders-Titans updates pop up on the screen. I know John sees them, too. And I know he must know I'm pretty excited. But he's not saying anything about it, and so neither am I.

Five minutes of game time later, the Chargers once again opt to go for it on fourth and short. This time it's a more sensible call. They're at the Patriots' 39 yard line, too far out for a field goal, too close in to punt. John's bothered by Schottenheimer's decision to go for it just the same, though.

"Now he's slapping us in the face," he tells me.

This time the Pats stop Tomlinson short of the first down. The Patriots are back in the game. And so is John.

"That's huge!" he yells, jumping to his feet, hands on his head. "That's huge!"

He turns to me.

"That's a huge play," he offers. "That's a game turner."

I hope he's right.

He isn't.

The Pats move to the Chargers' 23 yard line only to see Brady throw his second pick of the day. John's on his knees, head in his hands. "No! No! No!"

The Chargers can't capitalize on turnover, though. They move the ball well at first, only to stall out on the Patriots side of the field. And the fourth quarter opens with the Pats blocking a 50-yard field goal attempt.

John's excited, but he doesn't have nearly as much energy as he had before. He doesn't even get off the couch when the field goal is blocked. He just turns and shakes my hand again. He seems preoccupied.

A short time later, as the Chargers offense takes over after New England fails to convert on a fourth down, John lets me know what's on his mind. Watching Tomlinson rack up 177 yards in three quarters, he's started to wonder if harassing those Dolphins fans earlier in the day might not come back to haunt him sooner rather than later. The Pats will be visiting Miami in a week, and Ricky Williams, one of the best running backs in the game, awaits.

"Geez," John says. "You've gotta be worried about Williams next week regardless of what happens here."

What happens next is that the Patriots get the ball back on their own 14 yard line with just slightly more than eight minutes left to play. John thinks there's hope, though he's not nearly so sure of that as he'd like to be.

"Here we go," he says. "A patented Patriots five-minute drive for a touchdown, stop 'em and then kick the field goal to win it."

He pauses for a second, then looks at me. "Right?"

All I can say is, "I hope so."

Up the coast, my Raiders are ahead 38–25. That's closer than I'd like the score to be, but I'm certainly not about to look for any sympathy from John.

John's hopes for the Pats don't pan out. Their patented five-minute drive turns into a three-and-a-half-minute series of decent plays interspersed with penalties and incomplete passes.

The Pats get the ball back one more time just after the two-minute warning, but the drive that starts at their own 4 yard line ends when running back Kevin Faulk makes a foolish mistake, attempting to lateral to wide receiver David Patten, and gives the ball back to the Chargers at their 42.

San Diego takes a knee and the game ends with the score on the board unchanged since the beginning of the third quarter: Chargers 21, Patriots 14. Tomlinson has put up an astounding 217 yards on 27 carries, tying the single-game record for his team and raising all kinds of questions about the Patriots' defense.

John has very little to say. "That sucks the energy right out of you," he offers. The look on his face and the slump of his shoulders tell me he isn't speaking metaphorically.

He turns off the TV and thanks me for coming out to watch the game with him. As I head for the door, he smiles a warm, if deflated, smile and shrugs a "you can't win 'em all" shrug.

A few minutes later, as I drive past the airport scanning the radio for a final score on the Raiders-Titans game (the Raiders win it 52–31), I cross my toes in hopes there's nothing to worry about in Miami. And I cross my fingers in hopes that John will ultimately get what he deserves from the team he loves so much.

5.

Game 5 at Miami Dolphins

Sunday, October 6, 2002
Record 3–1

A tease is a bad bet. That's all I can think about as Gainer and I make the drive up from Dartmouth to New Bedford.

Gainer has a two-way tease on today's Patriots-Dolphins game. He's got the Pats getting nine points and the over at 38. He's going to lose. I know he's going to lose, because everyone always loses teases. But I couldn't begin to say which part of Gainer's tease is the loser.

I have a feeling the Pats may do better than cover the spread today. I have the idea that maybe they're going to win. I have a hope—no, more than a hope, a suspicion—that last week's loss in San Diego served as a wake-up call for Bill Belichick. And the Pats' head coach is a brilliant defensive strategist. So even though I still don't quite believe in the Patriots, I do believe that Belichick must have found a way to fix whatever was wrong with his team's run defense.

I think the Pats can stop Ricky Williams. And since stopping Williams amounts to stopping the Dolphins, I think the Pats can win.

The rest of the football-watching world—the part of it outside New England, anyhow—isn't quite so sure. The Pats' loss to the Chargers has dropped the Pats in ESPN.com's Power Rankings from number one to number three. Vegas has Miami giving three points this afternoon. And most of the national experts—in *Pro-Football Weekly,* on HBO, ESPN, the broadcast networks, and pretty much everywhere else—have picked Miami to win. Those guys know a whole lot more about football than I do. They must be onto something.

But Gainer doesn't appear to be in a whole lot of trouble there either way. Whether the Pats will lose is one thing; whether they'll lose by ten points or more is entirely another. Yeah, the Pats are coming in fresh off a frustrating road loss, but they're still 3–1 on the season. They've still won three tough games against good football teams. It's hard to imagine they'll lie down in a big match against a division rival.

Of course, Gainer doesn't necessarily seem to be in trouble with the over, either. He only needs to get a total of 38 points out of a couple of teams that have averaged just better than 32 points each in their games thus far this season.

But that's just the thing about teases. They fool you into believing you can't lose, when the truth is that you're almost certainly going to lose. Gainer doesn't simply need either the Pats to keep it within nine or the point total to top 38; he needs both of those things. And while there's no telling which, I know one side of Gainer's tease isn't going to go his way.

But I'm just thinking that. I'm not saying anything.

The game's already under way—we're listening to it on the radio, hearing the call of a missed field goal attempt by Miami's Olindo Mare as we drive down the street in New Bedford where Gainer's friend Rick lives—so it's not like it would be particularly helpful for me to make some comment at this point. Really, it never would have been. Gainer's a young guy, a 21-year-old college student and about as given to listening to reason as young men ever have been. Besides, I've known plenty of gamblers in my life—never the high rollers of legend, just an endless string of lottery junkies, casino bus trippers, and sports gamers. Coworkers, friends, and family members. I'm not entirely averse to putting a few dollars on a football game myself every once in a while, though I don't place a tenth as many bets as I think about placing (I'm ultimately too cheap and too chicken). So I know full well that there's no talking a gambler out of a bet once he's decided he's got the system beat.

And teases are attractive bets, even if they're not particularly smart.

Well, to be fair, all bets are attractive, and no bet is particularly smart. Everyone knows this. Even the most optimistic bettor recognizes it at some level. No one honestly believes bookies take bets and casinos stay in business because they love giving money to all those gamblers who are forever winning. (I should point out that the gamblers I've known have all been exceptions to this rule. Virtually every gambler I've ever met has claimed to be on the winning side of the equation.)

But teases are extra attractive. Indeed, they're probably the most attractive bets on the football gambler's menu. There are two reasons for this. First, with a tease there's typically no vig (the 10 percent surcharge you pay your bookie or the casino when you lose a straight bet). When you lose a tease, you pay the amount you wagered and that's that. Second, teases give bettors the chance to monkey with point spreads and over-under lines, adding or subtracting points in whatever manner suits their fancy. Thus, a tease plays on the bettor's ego and provides a false sense of security.

Of course, both of those factors only confirm that a tease is a sucker bet. In gambling, as in all aspects of life, anything that looks too good to be true is surely the bait in someone's trap. But, again, there's simply no way of getting a determined gambler to acknowledge any truth that stands between him and his imaginary pot of gold. So teases are wagered and lost all over America every weekend during football season.

There are a handful of ways to gamble on a professional football game. The one that's probably best known is the straight bet against the line. And, in fact, the handicappers' line is a factor in most forms of football gambling.

The line, or spread, on any particular game is a reflection of handicappers' assessment of the two teams and the conditions under which they're playing. Oddsmakers look at factors that go beyond the teams' records. They consider how each team's offense matches up against the other's defense (a team with a great running back, for example, looks good going up against a team with a horrible run defense). They look at key injuries. They look at whose stadium the game will take place in and what the weather will be like. And they use that data to establish a point spread, essentially a mechanism for spotting the underdog team a number of points.

So when you bet against the line, if you bet the favorite, you're picking it to post more points than the underdog's total score plus the spread. Bet the underdog and you're saying you think their total plus the spread will exceed the favorite's actual total score. Adjust the final score by the line (either by adding the amount of the spread to the underdog's score or by subtracting it from the favorite's) and you have the outcome vs. the line.

The other number handicappers establish for each game is the over-under line. The over-under reflects the total points oddsmakers think will be scored by both teams. You bet over if you think the actual total will be more than the over-under line, under if you think it'll be less.

Both the spread and the over-under can be used to place straight bets (i.e., bets that depend on one particular outcome of a game—the favorite to outscore the spread, for instance, or the two teams to combine for more points in the over-under), which ostensibly give the bettor an even chance of winning. So they should pay even money. Bet against the line with a friend from work and you're making an even-money bet.

But bookies and casinos don't like 50–50 odds. Even money doesn't keep them in business. So they take more on losing bets than they pay out to winners. With straight bets, they accomplish this by charging losers a 10 percent bump (the vig) on their wagers. So in reality, when you place a straight bet with a pro, you have to risk $110 for a chance to win $100.

If you don't want to pay vig, you've got three ways to go.

You can bet the money line, where you get a fairly standard type of odds, the kind where the bookie essentially promises to pay, for example, $2 for every $1 you wager if things go your way. Say the money line is the Pats +150; that means if you bet $100 on the Patriots and they win, you collect $150. The odds in that scenario are three to two against a Patriots win (i.e., you win $3 for every $2 you bet). If the money line were Pats −150, you'd have to risk $150 for a chance to win $100; you'd be getting three to two in favor of the Pats (you win $2 for every $3 you bet).

Here, the bookie ensures himself a win by laying different odds on the potential outcomes of the games, so he's always going to take more from losers than he pays out to winners.

You can also bet a parlay, where you pick more than one game against the spread, and you have to win all your games to win the wager. People who play a weekly football card are betting parlays. A parlay is attractive because you can win $100 (usually more) on a bet of $50. But parlays only pay well because they're low-percentage bets. Every game you add to a parlay increases your potential payout, but not by nearly as much as it decreases your chances of winning. Bookies probably collect on 20 or more parlays for every one they pay out.

And, of course, you can bet a tease.

It's called a tease because they tease you by allowing you to stroke the spread or the over-under by a set number of points. How many depends on how many different elements you add to your tease. You need at least two parts to a tease, and in a two-way tease you typically get six points to play with on each bet. You can tease either the betting line or the over-under in each of two games. Or you can tease both lines in a single game. In Gainer's case, he's teased both the spread and the over-under on the Pats-Dolphins. With the Pats getting three points in the straight-betting line, he's opted to give them the extra six. So he's got the Pats getting nine. And the over-under is 44; he's teased it down to 38 and bet over.

It seems like a decent bet, since the oddsmakers think the Pats will lose by only three, and the total score will top 44. But it isn't a good bet. Because teases are never good bets. That's why there's no vig; your odds of winning both ways are astronomically low.

It all comes down to this: Gainer was screwed before kickoff. So was his buddy Doug, who also has the Patriots getting nine but has paired it with a teased-down over-under on the Arizona-Carolina game. So was just about every one of the young gamblers we're going to hang out with at Rick's place. Because they've all got some action on some game today.

I keep thinking about this sociology professor I had back when I was in college who would say over and over, "Gambling is losing." He wasn't actually out to dissuade his students from gambling. He just used gambling to illustrate his belief in the importance of watching statistics. But he was still right.

Another thing about gambling, though, is that it really does have a way of making professional football more exciting.

* * *

Football is a beautiful and exciting sport to watch. The skill, the athleticism, the strategy involved are all engrossing. The sight of a great running back twirling his way through a crowd of would-be tacklers with balletic precision and then turning on bewildering speed as he breaks into the open field will stop a conversation dead. Watching a wide receiver pull in a fingertip grab as he sails through the air or skitter along the sideline just inbounds as he pulls in a pass can just about stop your heart.

The trouble though is that, contrary to the perceptions of many a fan's spouse, there isn't always a football game on. Indeed, NFL games are played pretty much all at once. You can't watch a pro football game or two every day of the week. You've got 12 or 14 of them coming at you in two big batches on a Sunday afternoon, which can make it hard to appreciate a lot of the skill, athleticism, and strategy. And, especially early in the season when it's all but impossible to get your head around how the outcomes of most games could affect the play-offs, it can be damned difficult to care about a lot of games unless you've got some personal stake in them.

A lot of fans make game days more exciting the cheap and easy way—by getting into office pools. Most pools are based strictly on straight-ahead picking; everyone picks all 16 games and the player who picks the most winners takes the prize. You don't even need to follow the league to play. (In fact, there's at least one week in every season, upset week, in which the whole league gets turned on its head and the key to winning your office pool is not knowing anything about football.) Better still, a pool might run you $5 a week. So while winning an office football pool never set anyone up to take an early retirement, neither did losing one ever force anyone into bankruptcy. Dollar for dollar, office pools are your best sports-gaming value.

But a pool isn't quite enough for fans like Gainer and his pals. They need the stakes to be higher, if only marginally. And, more important, they need more involvement in their action than a pool offers. They want to end the day a little richer, but they mostly want to end the day feeling like they really know football.

The folks I'm with today—there are seven of them all together, five men and two women—are all students at the University of

Massachusetts, Dartmouth. They're not trust-fund kids, just plain old poor-as-dirt college students. So the stakes aren't exactly staggering. Twenty-five-dollar teases seem to be the standard. It's enough to keep things interesting without draining anyone's tuition fund.

Small-stakes betting is also easier for them to do than the big stuff would be. They're not placing their bets with some crooked-nosed Cosa Nostra associate (not directly, anyhow). There's just some kid in the dorms who takes their action. He's got a connection to a guy he can place a bigger bet with for you if you want, but most of the time no one wants that.

Gainer says most of the gamblers gathered at Rick's have some kind of bet going every weekend. He swears some of them actually win sometimes. But he's an honest kind of guy, so he doesn't make any claims about anyone being in the black for the season.

The thing I don't quite understand at first is why Gainer and his friends bet on their own team. These are Patriots fans. The way I look at the utility of gambling is that it would make more sense for them to put their money on another team, since they've already got a reason to care about the Pats game. There's also the fact that betting on your own team is usually even less wise than betting in general. There are enough factors to consider when wagering on football without fan loyalties clouding your vision.

But it doesn't take terribly long for me to learn the strategy behind betting on the Pats.

The eight of us have been crowded into the tiny living room at Rick's very-student apartment—hippie tapestry on the wall, flower beads over the built-in bookshelves; massive four-hose hookah on top of the TV—for only a few minutes when Tom Brady loses a fumble, which the Dolphins cover at the Pats' 39 yard line. Curses go around the room.

Then Gainer, sheepishly but substantially less under his breath than he pretends to have hoped, reveals that he's not entirely disappointed to see Miami get good field position. "Part of me wants the points." Of course he does. Every score that goes up on the board gets him closer to hitting the over.

Mark, who's sitting next to Gainer on a beat-up couch, takes issue without taking his eyes off the TV set. Mark has the over, too, but he's still not ready to start rooting for Miami to score—not this early in the game.

"I want the points, but I don't want the Patriots to lose," Mark says in a stern tone intended to remind Gainer that the bet is supposed to come after the team.

Gainer doesn't want anyone getting the wrong idea. "Hey, hey. I don't want the Patriots to lose," he offers, then, after a short pause, "All I'm saying is I wouldn't mind the points."

The Dolphins spend a ridiculous amount of game time, more than five minutes, moving from the 39 to the 10 yard line, from which point they'll get three chances to score the first touchdown of the game. Gainer again exhibits his ambivalence. "They're gonna punch it in right here. It's gonna be seven points," he says with more than a hint of distaste. But a grin comes over his face as he changes his tone for an aside: "Not that that's necessarily a bad thing."

This time Mark does take his eyes off the set, though just long enough to glare at Gainer.

As I watch Miami quarterback Jay Fiedler carry the ball eight yards into the end zone on third down, I think about how in some circles Gainer's disloyal statements would be considered unforgivable. Here, they're understood. The people in Rick's living room may be Pats fans, I realize, but they're not diehards. They're just kids who like the team.

Gainer's pals are standard Patriots fans in at least one regard. They've got the gloom-and-doom bit down.

Early in the second quarter Brady foolishly decides to throw into a pack of Dolphins defensive backs on third and 11. Cornerback Patrick Surtain pulls down the interception. And Rick feels like he's been here before.

"Here he goes," Rick says, sounding 21 going on 50. "What's that, three interceptions in the last two games?"

"Don't turn on Brady now," warns Mark, clearly the closest thing to a true Pats loyalist in the room.

But Rick's got his head in that negative space to which Patriots fans are naturally drawn. He mentions his plans to travel to Buffalo for the Pats-Bills game on November 3. It will be the first time the Patriots square off against the team now led by their former quarterback Drew Bledsoe.

Not everyone in New England is certain it was a good idea to let Bledsoe go in favor of Brady. And on a day like today, with Brady struggling, fan fondness for the old QB is bound to be at its height.

"I'm not gonna know who to root for in Buffalo," Rick announces.

Mark's been here before, too, it seems.

"Typical Boston fan," he mutters. He's sunk back into the couch as the Pats' fortunes have faded so I can't see him from where I'm sitting. But in my mind he's got his eyes cast downward and he's shaking his head in disgust.

Things don't get any better any time soon.

The Dolphins go up 13–0 on the drive that follows the Surtain interception. They force the Pats to punt four plays later and nail a 26-yard punt return, which sets the Fins up to start a drive at midfield.

Now Gainer makes it official. Hes about done with being excited about the Pats for today.

"The Sopranos should be good tonight, huh?"

I can actually feel my head swing around as I turn to glare at him. I'm not alone. No one's winning their bets and the Pats aren't winning their game. Tensions are high. No one's really interested in laughing.

But Gainer's the kind of guy who trades in levity—regardless of whether it's welcome. He's not cowed by a roomful of dirty looks.

"Well," he says with a grin, "that's something."

If nothing else, it gives me another glimpse at how this crowd approaches gambling. They'll gamble on anything.

Gainer's comment reopens what is obviously an old discussion about whether Joe Pantoliano's character, Ralph Cifaretto, is going to be killed on tonight's episode. Mark and Doug have a bet on it.

Mark's got his money on Ralph getting dead. And he's got reasons.

"It's a mob show and nobody's gotten killed in a while," Mark says.

"So that means Ralph's getting killed?" Doug challenges.

Mark doesn't miss a step. "Pantoliano's got a book out. He's doing the talk shows."

None of that stuff necessarily points to a hit on Ralph (who'll end up surviving another few weeks yet), but it does point to the way a gambler's mind works. Mark figures he's got an angle and he's gonna do what he can to work it for a few bucks.

As it turns out, those bets on the game do serve a purpose today. They keep some excitement in the room even as the game goes horribly for the Patriots.

At halftime, the score stands at 16–0. The Pats aren't getting trampled by Ricky Williams the way they got trampled by LaDainian Tomlinson in San Diego, but they aren't exactly shutting Williams down either; he has a respectable 53 yards to his credit.

The hookah comes down off the TV and the mood of the room gets an artificial boost. But even that doesn't really erase the sourness of the day. It's hard, even for a crowd of semicommitted fans and one outright nonbeliever, to watch the home team fall apart the way the Pats have fallen apart in this game.

This isn't like the Chargers game a week ago. The Pats were never out of that game until the very end. They've been out of this one since sometime shortly after the very beginning.

As the third quarter gets under way, I start to think about that game in Buffalo, a game to which I'll be traveling, too. I also start to wonder about what's on tap between now and then. After today, the Pats head back to Foxborough, where they'll host Green Bay and, after their bye week, Denver, two teams with good records and great running backs.

It's looking like the Pats are headed for 3–2. And given the way the Kansas City game went, it's not unfair to say the Pats are a coin toss away from 2–3. There's no question but that the Patriots have to beat the Packers and Broncos. If they can go into Buffalo 5–2, they'll look like they're back on track and headed for the play-offs. But if they're 3–4 heading into that game, it's going to be a long trip, and quite possibly a long season.

The Patriots put up a touchdown in the third quarter, but they try a two-point conversion and miss, killing what little wind the score might have put into New England's sails. And the Dolphins quickly match the TD, extending their lead slightly by way of the extra point.

When the Pats score a second touchdown and pull within 10 points late in the fourth quarter, there's little reason to cheer. It's much too little, much too late. But Gainer, at least, is still excited. The score is 23–13. That puts him within one more Patriots score of covering both sides of his tease. And while it seems unlikely the Pats will produce anything more today, there are close to five minutes of game time left. Anything is possible.

Doug's possibilities in this game are slightly better—he just needs another score; which team gets it is immaterial—but it doesn't matter. Arizona and Carolina aren't going to top the over in their game, which will knock Doug out of his tease.

Mark's getting half of his tease courtesy of my Raiders, who are on their way to putting up 49 points in their game against the Bills. But he, too, needs the Pats to keep it within 9.

No one else is talking about their bets any more, which leads me to assume they've got nothing good to report.

A Miami field goal gives Gainer his over, but it leaves only a minute and a half on the clock.

"If the Pats score a touchdown, I'll be okay," Mark notes.

Doug and Rick want to know what happened to the Pats fan who'd scolded others for putting their wagers first earlier in the day.

"You'll be okay?" Doug asks.

"You can't be happy," Rick says.

"No," Mark answers, "but I'm gonna feel a lot happier if they lose 26–20."

It's just been that kind of day.

The Patriots never get that last score. They turn the ball over on downs, wrapping up a truly miserable performance with yet another ineffective drive. As the Dolphins run out the clock, no one's happy. This day's been nothing but a big, thick, heavy disappointment all around.

We stay long enough to see Doug lose the second half of his tease as Arizona edges Carolina by a score of 16–13. Then we're on our way.

Walking out the front door of Rick's building, Gainer asks, "Can you believe how depressing it is in there?"

"It's pretty bad," I say.

"I had to get out of there."

"Let me ask you this," I say, just wanting to make sure I haven't missed something. "Did anybody win any money in there today?"

"No," Gainer says, laughing. "Everybody lost today."

6.

Game 6 vs. Green Bay Packers

Sunday, October 13, 2002
Record 3–2

Everything is familiar. Not all of it is miserable.

Soft, steady rain on a day too warm for mid-October is entirely familiar. And although it's certainly not the glorious autumn weather everyone craves, it's anything but miserable.

In fact, the rain makes a game of two-hand touch seem more . . . I'm not sure. Authentic, maybe. Or perhaps just less frivolous. Football is supposed to be a little muddy, even backyard football, even when you're probably just slightly too old for such things. A little rain and a wet yard make it feel like you must be playing for some reason, something more serious than the simple fact that someone brought a ball.

This house and this yard have become familiar by now. I've spent maybe a dozen game days here since my buddy Tom bought the place two years ago. I've driven the winding road through acres of Douglas, Massachusetts, woodlands to get here on several occasions when there was no game to watch, too.

The big side yard has served as the field for enough Wiffle-ball games that I don't need to look anymore to know how close I am to where the lawn drops off in a steep slope down to the street.

I've already got a good idea of where I'll sit, come game time, in the narrow living room that always makes me wonder why so many of the big, new homes you see these days are designed with such awkward little spaces for entertaining. (The answer, I know, is that these new construction colonials are structured to keep their owners adding on. You're supposed to put on an attached two-car garage. And you're supposed to finish the space above the garage to serve as what they call a great room. But there's no garage here at Tom's house. There's no great room. And their absence only makes me ponder the cynicism of developers who design expensive new homes to feel incomplete.)

The guys I'm spending this game day with are certainly familiar. Of the half-dozen friends I'm hanging out with today, there's only one, Whitey, whom I've known for less than 22 years.

I've known Tom, the host, for 31 years. I guess we became friends mostly because our parents knew each other. Tom's father and mine worked together for what was then Bell Telephone. And then Tom's parents and mine built their first houses in the same suburban subdivision in Milford, Massachusetts, 20 minutes or so down Route 16 from where we are now. So Tom and I were thrown together in that odd way that parents throw kids together without much to go on other than the fact that they're both five-year-old boys. Most of the time, those kinds of friendships don't last much past the first grade. But in our case, it just somehow stuck.

I've known Chris for slightly longer than Tom. Thirty-three years. We were thrown together, too, I suppose. The way I remember it (assuming I really remember it at all; you're not supposed to remember anything that happened to you much before the age of three) my folks just sort of brought Chris home one day. And what are you going to do but love your baby brother?

There's John, Dave, and Bob, all three of whom I got to know in our freshman year at Milford High School in 1980.

I don't see Dave all that often these days. Haven't, really, since he got married more than a decade ago. But even though we've seen each other maybe twice a year since then, there's never any need for us to get reacquainted. Old familiarity is enduring familiarity.

John was one of the guys who went along with me on my trek to Manhattan for the Jets game. I haven't seen him since then. It's been a bit longer since I last hung out with Bob, but only by a matter of weeks. Whenever I was here at Tom's house last, for Wiffle ball, beer, and burgers on the grill, Bob was on hand, too. John and Bob are the guys—along with Tom, Chris, and another old friend, Ken, who's at the game in Foxborough today—who stood up at my wedding. People don't get any more familiar than that.

And, hell, you know, even Whitey, who's mostly Bob's pal and whom I typically see only once a year, at Bob's annual Christmas party, I've known for a good 15 years.

Oh, and there's Riley. I've known Riley only since 2000, but that still adds up to 14 dog years. Plus, Riley gets a special dispensation because he's a touch-football ace in the hole. You pretend to know a fellow like Riley better than you do, because you want him on your team. He's not worth a damn on offense—he can neither throw, catch, nor carry a football—but he plays a mean all-around defender, rushing the line like an end, then dropping back into pass coverage like the most blazingly fast cornerback in the league as soon as the ball is thrown. He's the four-legged linebacker of the future.

I'm perfectly familiar with the ways in which all these guys approach pro football. Like me, they're fans of the game before they're anything else. Most of us can watch any football game, any time, and be happy.

These guys are also Patriots fans. But they're Pats fans either in the way I've always known Pats fans or in the way I've always been a Pats fan. That is, some of them are always loyal to the Pats, but are careful, most years, to let you know they don't expect much from their team, while others support the Pats because they're the home team, but care more about whatever other team they grew to like as kids, when it was too hard to put the Patriots first.

Tom's a Denver Broncos fan, a fact that can contribute to a certain amount of tension between us. His Broncos and my Raiders don't much care for each other. They're bitter division rivals. And it's not infrequent that they end a season competing for the AFC West title or a wild card slot on the play-offs.

While we both try to be civil about the rivalry, neither Tom nor I makes any effort to conceal our glee at the good fortune of our own team or the misfortune of the other's. If we weren't such good friends, we'd probably hate each other.

Bob's a Pats fan before anything else. But he's not bragging about that to anyone just now. Indeed, today he's decked out in Minnesota Vikings gear—a game jersey and baseball cap. (Bob claims he just likes Vikings purple, and I have to believe him given the circumstances of the current season. While it hasn't been easy to support the Patriots over the last couple of weeks, this really isn't a good year even to pretend to be a Vikings fan.) In all the years I've known Bob, I've never once heard him make a positive prediction about the Pats' chances heading into a season, or so much as a game. Of course, that may not have much to do with the Pats. Bob is one of those people who always expects the worst in any situation.

Dave and John don't root for anyone but the Pats. But they don't talk about football much; while both are fans of the game, neither of them lives for football the way Tom and I do. John's been to Patriots games with the rest of us over the years, but I've never known him to get worked up about a win or to moan about a loss. When Dave isn't working or spending time with his wife and kids, he concentrates on music. He gave up any dreams of rock stardom years ago, but he still gets a lot of joy out of playing guitar and writing songs. That doesn't leave much time to be crazed about a football team. So his support for the Pats is largely passive—and enviably relaxed.

Chris doesn't really root for any team; he roots for himself. He participates in an office pool (through me) and his loyalties extend exactly as far as his weekly picks. He's happy when he can pick the Pats to win, but he doesn't apologize when he ends up pulling for the opposition, which is just what he'll be doing today.

Whitey always roots for the Pats, but today he's a bit preoccupied. Today, he's mostly interested in rooting for the Houston Texans to beat the Buffalo Bills. Whitey's angry about having been knocked out of his office's elimination-style loser pool (every week, you pick a team you believe is sure to lose; if you're right, you move on; if you're wrong, you're out; and the last player standing takes the pot). And what he's most interested in seeing now is whatever outcomes from around the league will hurt those still in contention. A lot of those folks have heavy underdog Houston as their loser this week. So Whitey's looking for the Texans to upset the Bills.

My brother all but bursts with delight as Whitey explains why he can't keep his mind on the Pats game.

"Spite!" Chris yells jubilantly. "God bless ya, man."

It's a familiar sentiment, and one I understand isn't intended as a joke. Chris is the kind of guy who finds Charlie and Marilyn Manson equally fascinating, who loves Coen Brothers films and fart jokes. He is a guy with a deep appreciation for perverse mental processes.

We gather at Tom's house early. Chris and I are the first to arrive, just after 11 A.M. The others show up not long after.

We crack open our first beers of the day and break out the football. We start out just playing catch, which presently becomes a game of keep away from Riley. The big chocolate Lab, still not much more than a pup, can't help but covet the ball. He's all over you when you're holding it. But when one of the humans messes up and the ball hits the ground, Riley hasn't the foggiest idea what to do with it. He can't get it in his mouth. He can't keep his forepaws balanced on it. He really can't do anything but stand by, head cocked, as whoever gets to him first snatches his prize away. But all is forgiven immediately once the pigskin is heaved back into play.

Once there are enough of us for a game of three on three (John, who prefers his Sundays on the mellow side, sits out), Tom puts Riley in the house and we break up into teams and get down to business.

We play two-hand touch on a field that stretches from a small stand of trees near Tom's toolshed in the backyard to the post that holds a birdhouse in the front, just short of where the slope to the street begins.

We run as hard as we can and throw as far as we can. We take plenty of breaks for laughing and breath catching and feeling the rain on our faces. We play for a just a little more than an hour. We tease each other with the ease that comes with familiarity. We get wet. Some of us get muddy. Then we head inside just in time for kickoff. And it's no time—not even long enough to shake off the damp—before the Patriots start to look familiar, too.

Only, with the Pats, the familiarity we encounter isn't of the comforting variety. It's a kind of familiarity that predates last season, a kind of familiarity that makes us feel uncomfortable in our muddy clothes. It's a kind of familiarity that is nothing short of miserable.

* * *

The Pats win the coin toss. It's one of the few things they'll get right all day. They start their opening drive at their 20 yard line and move the ball up to the Green Bay 43 with a series of nicely executed short passes and a pair of solid running plays. Then they abandon what's working and try to grab a seven-point lead all at once. Tom Brady underthrows David Patten on a deep route down the sideline and cornerback Bryant Westbrook makes a nice interception.

The Patriots get one more chance to score in the first quarter after the Packers offense struggles on the wet field. But New England has no better luck overcoming the weather and has to punt the ball away with seconds remaining.

And although you never expect a team to do much on offense in the first quarter of an NFL game, it feels like there's something nasty afoot. It feels distinctly like the Pats are hunting for a third straight loss.

Dave, however, is looking for a way to cut the team a break.

"I think it has to be hard to play in the rain like that," Dave says.

Chris, who played a few years of Pop Warner ball as a kid, reaches back into his memory just far enough to affect expertise. "It's really hard to play in the rain," he tells Dave. Then, "It was hard in the backyard league earlier."

"These guys aren't in the backyard league," I snap, annoyed about having to watch bad football. "They're supposed to be pros."

"Yeah," Dave says, smirking, eager, as usual, to get me wound up, "but I still think it has to be hard."

By a third of the way through the second quarter, we've all expressed our distaste for Cris Collinsworth, who's in the Fox-TV announcers booth today. We've already grown weary of Collinsworth's constant harping on the home team.

Although the game is scoreless, Collinsworth thinks the Pats are being outplayed. Green Bay running back Ahman Green has managed 28 yards on seven carries so far today, but Collinsworth thinks the Pats' run defense is looking shaky. He's critical of the Pats' offensive strategy, which he thinks is putting too little emphasis on the ground game.

And the worst part of it all is that he's right about all of it. There's no quantifying the effects of a vibe on a football game, but there's a clear pro-Packers vibe in the air today. The 4–1 Packers clearly have come into Foxborough intent on notching their fifth win of the season. The 3–2 Pats look like they're still not quite sure what's hit them since they last played at home three weeks ago.

The fact of the matter is that 28 yards on seven carries averages out to four yards per run, more than enough to get the job done. And the Pats' run defense, which has given up more than 100 yards in each of the last three games, doesn't appear to be zeroing in on Green. Plus, the Pats are definitely passing too much. Whether that's only because they don't have a great running back to turn to on a day like this is irrelevant.

No one minds when one of the other guys points this stuff out. But no one wants to hear it from Collinsworth. That's because our negativity arises from frustration. His is objective. And it's paired with objective praise for Green Bay. And together, at least as we read it in our current state of mind, those two elements combine to make the way he's deriding the Pats seem joyful.

There's also the fact that none of us cared much for Collinsworth coming into this afternoon.

All of us—even Chris, who doesn't care what the guy has been saying about the Pats—think Collinsworth comes off as a good deal too self-satisfied. "He knows football," Whitey concedes, "but he's such an asshole." We agree that HBO's *Inside the NFL* isn't as good as it used to be now that Collinsworth and Bob Costas are hosting instead of Len Dawson and Nick Buoniconti (even though we all know it's actually better). We don't like Collinsworth's stupid, smug grin. We don't like his square head or his boxy haircut either.

After a lot of punting back and forth, the Pats manage to score first. Adam Vinatieri nails a 32-yard field goal five and a half minutes into the second quarter to put New England ahead 3–0.

But the Packers move the ball down the field fluidly on their next possession. Green picks up 11 yards on each of two consecutive carries. Brett Favre is hitting short- and midrange passes.

The Patriots offense, meanwhile, has been unable to move the ball much at all. Tom Brady is making mistakes no one would ever have tolerated from Drew Bledsoe, throwing the ball at defensive backs like he's shopping for interceptions and missing his receivers left and right. The defense isn't doing much better. And the team is committing too many penalties on both sides of the ball.

By the time the Packers complete a 76-yard drive to go up 7–3 toward the end of the half, we've all got a feeling it's the beginning of the end.

Chris is the only one who's happy about that. "Zip-a-dee-doo-dah," he shouts as Green Bay's placekicker, Ryan Longwell, puts up the extra point. "That's seven points for Green Bay."

No one gives him a hard time about it, mostly because we know it wouldn't help anything.

The Pats keep the ball for all of two plays after the kickoff. Then Kevin Faulk lets a backward pass from Brady drop to the ground and the Packers recover at New England's eight yard line. A quick toss from Favre to Green and the Pack is up by 11.

Chris and Bob, who are trying to remember the name of the old cartoon superheroes who included Tornado Man and Diaper Man (turns out they were on *The Mighty Heroes*), break away from their distraction only briefly to take note of the score.

"Fourteen to three?" Chris says with a tone of mock surprise. "I know where this one's going."

The rest of us just grumble. We know where it's going, too.

Yes, it's 14–3. But it's not nearly that close. The Patriots get the ball back and go nowhere with it once again. Then Brady throws another pick. We sit there watching, mostly in silence for a little while, then we get up and put our shoes on as the last seconds of the half tick off the clock. No one mentions the game, not even once, during our quick halftime round of backyard touch.

No one mentions the game much through most of the third quarter either. We all just sort of sit there and watch. None of us seriously believes the Pats will be able to come back and win the game. We all hope we're wrong, but there's no point in expecting anything. We've all had a lifetime to learn that lesson.

The Pats who started this season looking like they just might repeat as Super Bowl champions have disappeared. The Pats we're watching today are the Pats we've always known, clumsy and prone to error, talented but unable to put their talent to anything approaching effective use.

It's hard to say where these old Patriots came from. In reality, we never quite knew where they'd gone. Super Bowl XXXVI came almost out of nowhere, rounding out a season that began with the loss of Bledsoe to an injury and a dire outlook for the team. Then the Pats, led by Brady, just kept rolling, making it seem like the old days really might be gone. And that, of course, is how a team like the Pats sucks you in. Now, it appears, fate knows the team has won the maximum number of hearts. So now must be the time to start breaking them.

Late in the third quarter, as Tom Brady stands on the sideline—the usual cool confidence gone from his eyes, replaced with a bewilderment that says everything about his performance in this game—the Packers push the Pats defense down the field 92 yards in six plays. They set up on the Patriots' two yard line.

"What's that, 21?" Chris taunts.

"It will be any second," I mutter.

And it is. Tight end Bubba Franks catches Favre's third touchdown pass of the day, and Longwell adds the extra point.

"Oh, boy, guys, what happened today?" Chris says as he heads to the fridge. His back turned to the living room, he produces a fake, taunting laugh fit for a school yard: "Har, Har, Har!"

The third quarter is close to ending and so is our patience.

"That soccer team is the best team playing in Gillette Stadium right now," Whitey says. When you hear praise for a soccer team coming from a football fan, you know things are looking grim.

"They'll never win now," Bob says.

Whitey has an idea. He thinks maybe the Pats should switch to a hurry-up style. "They've gotta go with the two-minute offense," he says.

"Yeah," Bob says sarcastically. "That'll help."

We don't stop watching, though. We're hurt, but we're content to sit and press this bruise for a while.

We don't stop watching when Brady throws his third interception with two minutes remaining in the third.

We don't even stop watching three minutes into the fourth when Green plunges in for a fourth Packers touchdown. Not entirely, anyhow. We leave the game on even as a second TV comes out and we set up Tom's Nintendo for a game of *Super Mario Cart*.

By the time Brady and the Pats finally get it together and score their first touchdown with six minutes left in the game, the guys who aren't playing Nintendo have moved back out into the rain. It's sloppy out there now. And the overcast is bringing on an early dusk. But falling down in the muck is a lot more fun than watching the Pats do it.

Riley, who's been left inside, is running back and forth between windows, barking mightily at the ball, forgetting that he could never catch it even if he could get outside.

I know Tom wants the dog to stay inside, out of the rain, but I'm worried that Riley's going to trip over the Nintendo set and ruin our game. So I get up to let him out, shrugging at John, who's sitting on the couch, arms crossed, kind of zoning out.

I open the sliding glass door from the kitchen to the back porch and watch Riley burst out and down the short staircase to the yard. Then I listen to the shouts of "Oh, no" that rise up as Riley bounds across the yard, eager to play some D.

I sit back down and watch the Pats sputter a little more before I go back into videogame land. The guys outside are laughing as their game turns back to a round of keep away from Riley. They're in good spirits in spite of a miserable day for the Pats. So am I. Oakland's game against the St. Louis Rams is still coming up (though the Raiders will lose it). Tom, likewise, has Denver vs. Miami to look forward to (the Broncos will also lose).

My brother's still got a shot at the pool going into the late games.

And Whitey's outside, so he doesn't know the Bills have turned their game around and are beating Houston.

We've all been to this place, through these kinds of games, with the Patriots before—a lot more often than not.

My ability to believe in this team, what little of it I'd acquired over the first three weeks of the season, is gone. Not lessened, but simply gone. I can't imagine even the truest of the true believers isn't shaken after today. And since the Pats have their bye week coming up, we'll all have two weeks to ponder what has happened before the next game.

Except, perhaps, for Tom, my friends will still be rooting for the Pats when Denver gets to town on the 27th. So will I.

If this team wants to have any real shot at bouncing back and turning this into a winning season, it's going to need to close the month with a win over the Broncos. It's also going to have to go into Buffalo and beat the Bills November 3.

We'll continue to hope they'll pull it off, even if we can't be so sure anymore.

I can't speak for the other guys, but I have to admit that I kind of like the uncertainty. If nothing else, it's familiar.

7.

Game 7 vs. Denver Broncos

Sunday, October 27, 2002
Record 3-3

Even today, there are things that go as well as we could have hoped, that fit perfectly into the little slots we've carved out for them in our minds.

It's a football day. As pure and as perfect a football day, in fact, as anyone is likely to witness at Gillette Stadium this season. The sky is clear, the air cool heading for cold, rich with the scent of burgers and chicken that rises up from grills, gathers over the parking lots, then spreads out along Route 1.

Except for the fact that far too much of the foliage has yet to turn—robbing the horizon of color and the air of that vague scent of freshly fallen leaves that seems to hold autumn still even while announcing the turn toward winter—this is the kind of day that makes people fall in love with football in the first place.

There's no way to resist the charms of a day like this. The mild, punctuated breezes that play in your hair and send dry leaves dancing around your feet. The sunlight that shines warm and white on your face at noon, only to turn a mellow orange as the afternoon wears on. The calm that sets in with the approach of evening, creating the illusion that the world will always be exactly this way, allowing you to pretend you've forgotten about the hard, bitter months ahead.

And when you grow up with football, when your memories of these days are almost inextricably tied to the distant sounds of cheering and marching bands, you lose your ability to separate the season from the game.

I can't remember a time when fall wasn't in some way synonymous with football. My childhood memories of autumn are all filled with the game.

Even before my brother, the athletic kid in the family, took to playing for the town Pop Warner teams, fall Saturdays were football days. Dad always had the high school game on the radio as he worked in the yard or the garage. And on those Sundays when Mom had to work, Dad would keep an eye on the Patriots (or whatever game happened to be on TV) while he played silly games with my brother, my sister, and me.

I grew up within a short walk from Milford High School, and on weeks when there was a home game, our neighborhood would be filled with the sounds of drums and brass and the rhythms, though not the words, of the cheerleaders. Dad would take us to a game sometimes, too. We'd sit in the bleachers with him and do our best to follow a team we knew nothing about playing a game that's really too complicated for kids.

If there was a bit of winter in the air, Dad would buy himself a coffee and us kids hot chocolate. Standing near the concession stand, taking those first hot, sweet sips, I'd get caught up watching steam sneak out of our Styrofoam cups and swirl away into nowhere. The image of vapor leaving a cup of coffee to wander off into the cold air still fills me with the warmth of those memories.

After my brother started playing football and Dad started coaching, I'd spend Saturday afternoons on the sidelines. I can't say I watched much of my brother's games. Youth sports just aren't interesting unless you're one of the players or a player's parent. But the sounds of the game were there to color mornings and afternoons spent playing under the bleachers or just sitting on the grass reading.

We started going to Pats games when I was a bit older and could appreciate what I was seeing. We watched teams featuring Steve Grogan and Sam "Bam" Cunningham get beat up and down the field, but it didn't matter. We were out at the stadium watching a game.

I went to high school games regularly when I was at Milford High, though I can't say I remember watching too many of them. I never did see my college team play. My school, Worcester State

College, wasn't exactly known as a football power. Better to spend Saturdays watching the real college teams on TV.

And my friends and I almost always made it to at least one Pats game a season, even in those years when the team was at its worst. It didn't matter if the team was good or bad, nor that the stadium was a mess, because our trips to Foxborough were never nearly as much about the Pats as they were about the experience.

I can't separate fall from football. And I wouldn't if I could.

As Tom and I pull off Route 1 and search out a spot in the parking lot behind the End Zone bar, it's impossible not to think about the fact that this may be the only classic New England autumn day Patriots fans will get in Foxborough this year.

The Pats are back from their bye week, fresh and ready, we hope, for their game with the Denver Broncos. Bill Belichick has told the press the team spent its extra week getting back to basics. That seems like a very good idea. The Pats need to get some production out of an offense that lost its way in its last three games. They also need to find a way to stop the run on defense. They can't keep giving up 100-plus yards a game to running backs if they're going to get off the schneid.

After today, the Pats play three straight road games, tough ones, in Buffalo, Chicago, and Oakland. By the time they get back home to host Minnesota on November 24, the trees will be mostly bare. Thanksgiving will be nearing, keeping the idea of fall alive. But we'll all know winter is looming. They don't forecast this far ahead, but I'm sure no one will be at all surprised if it's raining one of those awful, late-November rains, the kind that soaks you then chills you to your core, ensuring you'll be sick just in time for the holiday.

So this is it. This has to be a big day for the Pats. Not just because they need it, not just because they've lost three straight coming in, nor because they may well lose two if not all three games on their extended road trip, but because we need it.

All of us gathered in the parking lots, the burger grillers by the backs of their cars; the prime-rib-and-mashed-potatoes types at the sides of their RVs; the low-key tailgaters, like Tom and me, with our cans of Bud, our sandwiches from the sausage guy, and our pregame show on the car radio. All of us walking up Route 1 to the stadium, still clutching a last beer, some shouting from time to time, some laughing loudly all the way. All of us crossing over the highway on the bridge, looking down on the sea of RVs in the stadium lot, watching their standards (Patriots banners and U.S. flags mostly, with an Irish flag here, a booze-company logo there) shift gently in the lazy breeze. We all need it.

I pause for a second just outside the stadium gates to chuckle at an assortment of fans sucking down the last mouthfuls of their final tailgate drinks. There's a line of stadium security staff members just ahead on the path to Gillette and just in front of them is an ever-growing mountain of empty beer cans.

I lose myself for a second as I listen to a young woman's voice from up ahead yelling, "Programs! Get your New England Patriots PRO-grams!" The call of stadium vendors always has a comforting sort of music about it.

Just after we walk past the program hawkers, Tom looks up at the stadium, glances down at his watch, and announces, "It's four o'clock."

He only means that the game's about to start, and his tone is just that flat, but coupled with the early and accelerating dusk, it causes me to swallow hard. The Patriots have to win today, I think, that's all there is to it.

As we walk toward the stadium gates, a cheer goes up from within. The people around us join in, though no one has any idea what they're cheering for. The excitement of the moment, the idea of a game about to start, is more than enough. Plus, it helps us use up some nervous energy.

Tom and I walk upward forever, ramp after ramp after endless ramp. We complete the climb to section 321. It's the highest up I've been in the new stadium. There's still one tier higher up than we are, but it's off to the sides (we're just about in the end zone). Behind us is a small plaza that reaches back to a cluster of concessions. We're in the last row, too, so there's certain to be guys standing behind us drinking and eating throughout the game.

We settle into our seats just in time for the coin toss. Denver calls it wrong, and I think maybe that's a good omen, maybe things will keep on going the Patriots' way.

* * *

My optimism is miserably short lived. The Pats fall flat on their first possession, punting after three ineffective plays nets them a lousy two yards. The Broncos, by contrast, make it look easy on their first drive. They go 52 yards in seven plays, scoring on a one-yard run by Clinton Portis.

The Pats get the ball back, lose two yards on three plays this time, and punt again.

Only the fact that Denver quarterback Brian Griese throws a downright stupid interception on the first play after the punt keeps any hope alive.

Brady completes his first two passes of the ensuing drive, hitting Troy Brown for 15, then Christian Fauria for nine. Then it's back to form for the Pats, who manage to get one yard out of their next five plays before they're forced to punt again.

Denver eats up the rest of the first quarter, then scores on an eight-yard Griese pass to tight end Shannon Sharpe to start the second.

Six plays and 15 yards of offense later, the Pats line up to punt once again.

Tom mutters, "This could get ugly."

There's only one thing I can possibly say in response: "So you don't think this is ugly already?"

Tom doesn't bother to answer. What he's thinking doesn't need saying.

Tom is a Denver fan before he's a Pats fan. Usually, anyhow. Today, he's rooting for the Pats, not just because we're at their stadium, but because he figures the Patriots need the win more. Tom's got a good bit of the cocky Broncos fan in him. He's dead certain his team will win its division, even if it is the toughest in the league (with San Diego, Kansas City, and Oakland all playing good football this season), so he's ready to give up a game to a home team whose chances of making the play-offs, much less repeating as league champs, are in serious jeopardy.

Still, Tom winces every time mistake-prone Griese holds the ball too long. And he casts smiling glances at the section full of Broncos fans behind us and to our left when his real team does well.

On the whole, the Broncos aren't looking especially good today. They're winning, yes, but by midway through the second quarter they've given up an interception and a fumble. Under a lot of circumstances, these turnovers would be causing the Broncos all kinds of problems. But under these circumstances, they're simply keeping the team from running away with the game.

The Pats, on the other hand, are looking particularly bad. Even when they turn that Denver fumble—a Rod Smith drop that's recovered by cornerback Ty Law at the Broncos' 42 yard line—into a short touchdown drive, they look awkward, halting in doing it. It doesn't inspire a renewal of anyone's confidence.

The Pats fans in this part of the stadium are mostly just quiet. They cheer for the odd good play, but mainly just sit, grumbling to themselves, occasionally grousing to their neighbors.

I don't hear a real jeer until late in the half, when Denver, having traveled 65 yards in six plays to set up on the Pats' 5 yard line, has a running play go for only a yard.

"Whooo-hoo!" comes a voice dripping with sarcasm, from just over my right shoulder. "We stopped 'em on that one!"

And all anyone within hearing distance can do is laugh.

It gets worse even before the half is out.

The Pats don't manage to stop the Broncos on their next play. Portis charges up the middle for a touchdown. Random and disjointed boos start to percolate up out of the crowd.

Then, on the Pats' first play after the Denver touchdown, Brady, who has looked worse today than in any of the three previous games, can't find a receiver and has to throw the ball away. Now the boos rise up from everywhere. And it's official: The hero of the Patriots 2001–02 season, and of Super Bowl XXXVI, the guy who took Drew Bledsoe's job and refused to give it back, is on his way to becoming this season's goat. He's already lost his mystique; he's now just another quarterback, the guy who's going to get blamed for every failure of his team's offense.

At the two-minute warning, I hear the utterance that I've known was inevitable since the moment the Pats' offense first started to slip in San Diego: "I knew trading Bledsoe to the Bills was gonna come back to haunt them."

I look over my left shoulder to see the speaker, a fat guy with a season ticket in a plastic envelope hanging from a lavaliere. I want to ask him if he was one of the people yelling for the team to dump Bledsoe after last season, but he looks angry enough already.

A pair of guys behind me and to my right—the pumpkin-headed fellow who got the negativity fest started with his mock enthusiasm moments earlier and his friend, a stumpy, round-shouldered guy in an ugly fleece pullover with a sort of southwestern pattern but in all the wrong colors (blue, purple, and green)—are insulting the team loudly and steadily. As the Pats line up to punt once again with seconds remaining in the half, Fat Guy looks over at his commiserators and offers, "These fuckin' losers don't even care. They'll sputter through the rest of the season."

He's off the mark, of course. The Pats may be struggling—or it might be worse than that; it could be that they're actually foundering—but it's not fair to assert that they don't care. I've been quick, over the years, to accuse the Patriots of fielding teams that didn't care about winning, but this isn't one of them. If they didn't care about winning, they'd have caved against Pittsburgh in week 1. No amount of residual momentum from Super Bowl XXXVI could have lifted a team that didn't care to a win that night. Moreover, if the Pats didn't care, they'd probably have been 0–6 coming into today.

I'm sure Fat Guy didn't really mean what he said. He's merely frustrated and engaging in hyperbole. But, still, I start to wonder what Louis, the true-hearted fan I met on opening night at the End Zone, would have to say if he were here. How would he react to the Gillette crowd turning on the Patriots just when the team could use their support most? How would he address a group of fans whose lack of faith is proving off-putting even to the steadfastly removed and skeptical likes of me.

"You nonbelievers," I hear Louis yelling in my head, "fuck you all!"

There are a few believers among us yet, however.

There's the youngish fellow in the big Patriots parka sitting two rows in front of us, for instance. He may have his doubts about the offense, but he continues to believe in the D.

At the start of the second half, as Denver threatens to score a touchdown that would surely put the game away, Parka Boy urges the section to rise and cheer on the defense with him. "Come on, D!" he yells at the top of his lungs, looking right, then left into the crowd, seeking support. "Come on!" He stretches his hands out, palms up, then jerks them upward several times in quick succession. He's attempting to conduct a symphony of cheers in support of the D. But no one here is up for playing that piece at the moment.

The Pats sack Griese for a big loss, bringing up third and 14 at New England's 35 yard line. It's probably the Patriots' best defensive play of the afternoon. It renders a Denver touchdown unlikely. Indeed, the Broncos will need to pick up a few yards just to get within reach of a long field goal.

Our one-man pep club looks around for high-fives, but gets only a few lackluster slaps from fans seated near him. Even those few whom he can guilt into offering their hands, however, just don't have it in them to stand up.

The nonbelievers in the concession area are completely unaffected by Parka Boy's enthusiasm.

"We're right back in it now," the guy in the bad pullover sneers when Jason Elam's 48-yard kick sails right of the uprights.

It's hard to fault the guy. His attitude may be wrong, but his assessment of the situation isn't.

The jeering section keeps it up through the next Patriots possession. Early in the drive, after offensive linemen Joe Andruzzi and Mike Compton commit dumb, costly penalties, Fat Guy has a bit of advice for the team.

"Don't break the rules!" he shouts. Clever.

The mood doesn't improve any after Adam Vinatieri nails a 26-yard field goal that cuts Denver's lead to 11, either.

"We've got 'em on the run now," Fat Guy quips. "Two more touchdowns and it's all over."

As Denver starts its next drive, Parka Boy once again tries to get section 321 into the action. "Come on!" he yells, looking around for help. "De-fense! De-fense! De-fense!"

He gets maybe half a dozen takers, including a woman sitting in front of Tom who joins in hesitantly and halfheartedly. I get the feeling she just sort of feels bad for the guy.

I realize that Tom's been quiet for a while and I start to wonder what's going on. Maybe he just doesn't know who to root for. Maybe he's stunned.

"What's up with you?" I ask. "At least your Broncos are gonna get a win."

Tom smiles and nods, then leans in closer to me. He pulls his hand up to his chest, uses his thumb to point, through him, to the scraggly bearded guy sitting on the other side of him. "This guy really, really smells," he whispers.

"Bad?" I ask.

"Really bad."

He turns back to watch the game and his neighbor, as if on cue, offers him some of his french fries. For once in this day, the oppressive atmosphere in Gillette actually comes in handy. It's the only thing that keeps the two of us from bursting into laughter.

Most of the way through the third quarter, Denver, leading 21–10, gets off a bad punt. The Patriots take possession at their 42 yard line.

Parka Boy is excited. "This is what we've waited for all day," he shouts.

Now I can't keep myself from jumping on the sarcasm wagon. I turn to Tom and ask, "It is?"

The Patriots do nothing with their good field position. And the two teams punt the ball back and forth through the rest of the quarter. The Pats manage a Brady-to-Fauria touchdown as the final period gets under way, but they blow the two-point conversion that would have brought them within a field goal of tying the game.

Even Parka Boy has gone quiet, now.

Pumpkinhead, on the other hand, has grown quite loud. "I'm ready," he says, responding to some unheard challenge. "I'm ready to go down and try to do better than these guys."

It isn't long thereafter, though, that he and Bad Pullover come up with a better plan. As Brady takes a sack that will bring on the punting team with just under 10 minutes left in the game, Pumpkinhead offers, "That's it." He and his friend turn to leave.

They aren't alone. Fall is turning to winter more quickly than anyone would have anticipated. It's grown fairly cold in Gillette

Stadium since sunset. And it appears there are few here willing to endure any amount of physical discomfort in order to support the Pats team we've seen on the field today.

Tom and I are among the few who stick it out until the final seconds of the game. I'm never quite sure why. What reason could we possibly have for staying here in the dark and cold of a late-October night to watch the Patriots lose a game they absolutely had to win?

When it's over, and the Pats have fallen 24–16, we make our way back down the endless sequence of ramps only to hit a bottleneck as we approach the gates. The scene is mostly quiet as fans file out of the stadium and head for the parking lots. But as we inch our way toward the gate, I hear a single, plaintive voice come up out of the crowd: "Bledsoe, where are you?"

It's only a week before the Pats travel to Buffalo, where Drew awaits. I might have tried to remind the yeller as much, but I'm pretty sure that's not what he meant.

8.

Game 8 at Buffalo Bills

Sunday, November 3, 2002
Record 3–4

It's hard to balance the happiness with the embarrassment. Almost as hard as it is to figure out how the idiots always manage to end up sitting in the back.

In certain situations, like on the bus, it makes sense. It feels natural. When you load 60 people onto a 60-passenger bus, someone's gonna end up sitting back near the can. The fact that the guys who will spend the trip drinking heavily, farting with juvenile pride, and loudly and continually asserting their homophobia and misogyny, almost invariably end up sitting in the rear only seems right. Sure, they're only trying to hide, engaging in behavior learned on school field trips to places they can't remember, but you can at least allow yourself to pretend their seating choice reveals that at some elemental level they understand where they belong.

In other situations, like today in Ralph Wilson Stadium, it's harder to explain. Most of the jackasses are gathered in the upper reaches of the facility, which leads me to believe there must be some kind of design at work. But it's difficult to believe that the Buffalo Bills box office somehow managed to identify the troublemakers from afar. And that leaves me to wonder how the buffoons ended up in the section of the stands that most resembles their natural habitat.

All I can figure is that there must be a pattern at work here. The Bills ticketers must have known something about the kind of people with whom Don and I have traveled to Buffalo for today's Patriots-Bills game. They must have learned from experience that a certain breed of fan is given to bad behavior. And I can only hope that the box office's ability to ID bad seeds from 450 miles away has to do with the type of people who take bus trips to football games and not with New England fans in general.

I've never been on one of these tours before—the ones offered by sports travel agencies, the ones that give you the chance to buy tickets, accommodations, and transportation all in a package. For all I know, the guys who sat in the back of our bus acting like animals the whole way across Massachusetts and upstate New York are exactly what you tend to get on these trips.

So it could be that the stadium knew where to put us just because they knew how we were getting our tickets. Or it could just be that these are the sections where block ticket buys are available, and that the rest is purely coincidental. Either way, it's worked out. Because we're in section 332, all the way up in the farthest reaches of the stadium. And a lot of the Pats fans sitting around us are . . . well, they're pretty much complete assholes.

It's funny: although I began the weekend with some concerns, none of them were about the trip. Nor were any about the way our traveling companions would behave once we got to the game. The only things I was worried about as I drove out to Auburn early Saturday morning to meet Don and the bus were how the Pats would fare in their first meeting with their former quarterback Drew Bledsoe and whether New England's season would have much meaning by the time we got back home.

Bledsoe had been famously sportsmanlike in the way he handled losing his job to Tom Brady the previous season. Knocked out for several weeks after he was injured during a loss to the Jets, Bledsoe recovered only to learn that Bill Belichick intended to keep starting Brady. And although he had done nothing to earn being benched (and despite the fact that there's an unwritten rule in pro football that you don't lose your starter status permanently as the result of an injury), Bledsoe took the demotion with the same class and maturity he displayed throughout his nine seasons with the team.

It couldn't have been easy for Bledsoe, who'd lost a Super Bowl to Green Bay in '97, to watch Brady lead the team to its first-ever league championship. It couldn't have been easy for him to ride out the 2001–02 season knowing he'd be headed elsewhere in

September 2002. But he did it. And when the trade to Buffalo was complete, he left without ever offering a cross word for Brady, Belichick, the Patriots, or the team's fans.

But none of that meant Bledsoe wouldn't be geared up to play the Pats for the first time. None of it meant he wouldn't be looking to show Belichick he'd made a mistake by sticking with Brady. And, certainly, none of it meant he wouldn't be looking to lead the Bills' extremely potent offense in a rout of his former team.

More frightening still, the Pats were looking very much like a team that could be routed. The tough squad that shoved victories down three solid opponents' throats to open the season had disappeared, replaced by a team that gave up 99 points and scored only 53 in the course of four straight losses. And they were headed to Buffalo to face a Bills team that was averaging 30 points a game and had a respectable 5–3 record.

The Pats claimed to be working to fix a run defense that had given up 100 or more yards to a single rusher in five consecutive games. And, of course, Brady would be looking to get back on track after posting a career-worst performance against Denver. But trying and seeking are different from doing. And the Pats simply hadn't been doing a whole lot of doing.

A loss to the Bills wouldn't officially end the Pats' season (week 9 is still a good bit early to be talking about elimination), but it would make the team's chances of securing a play-off berth appear distant at the very best. With the AFC East shaping up as one of the most competitive divisions in football, 3–5 wouldn't be a record anyone could feel comfortable with.

Those were the things I thought about as I drove out of Northampton at 5:30 Saturday morning. And they were still foremost on my mind an hour and a half later as I pulled into the hotel parking lot where we were to meet the bus.

There were already two dozen or so people hanging out in the lot when I arrived. Maybe two-thirds men. Some young, maybe early 20s. Some a few years older than me—late 30s or early 40s at the outside—but none much older than that. A bunch of them were lazily tossing a football around. Others stood by their cars, hands in their pockets, bouncing slightly at the knees the way you will when it's colder outside than you'd like it to be but not bitter enough to keep you trapped indoors. A lot of them had beer cans in their hands.

Don, whom I hadn't seen since our trip to Manhattan back when the Pats were still looking like world beaters, emerged from his car when he saw me pulling up.

He greeted me with his usual closed-mouthed smile and lazy nod. "Hey, buddy," he said. "You ready?"

There was a knowingness and a sense of mischief in his tone that told me the question was more than it seemed. I looked around at the crowd in the lot and thought about how Don must have been there watching them for a little while.

"These guys are drinking already?" I said, sounding a good bit more surprised than I really was.

Don, who can talk when he wants to but doesn't feel the need to verbalize his every thought, simply turned up his grin to the sly setting, angled his head back two degrees, nodded twice, and offered, "Yup."

"It's gonna be a long ride to Buffalo, isn't it?" I said.

This time I got one of Don's trademark short, sharp, I'm-with-you-buddy laughs. Then another "Yup."

The trip started out okay. The folks who boarded the bus with us in Auburn seemed a pleasant enough bunch. Even the ones who'd begun their drinking in the powdery first light of the day were fairly subdued. We stowed our bags, took our seats, and then met our bus driver and our chaperone.

Joe, a representative of the tour company that organized the trip, told us we were among 950 people his firm was taking to Buffalo for the game. Ours was bus 11. We needed to remember that, because Joe's company was sending 17 buses to the game, buses that were departing from a variety of locations in Massachusetts and would be returning to their points of departure. It would be a mistake to board the wrong bus on the way home.

Joe, who would be part of the bus 11 family for the entire trip to Buffalo, also took a second to let us know a little bit about himself and his feelings about the upcoming game. "I am a season ticket holder," he said. "We shouldn't have traded him."

Joe told us we had a handful of other passengers to pick up in Chicopee (a city not 20 minutes from Northampton; I wished someone at the travel agency had told me that was an option) and then we'd be heading straight out across New York, making two pit stops on the New York State Thruway.

Sid, our bus driver, asked us to keep the bus clean and wished us an enjoyable trip. And then we were on our way to Chicopee, which is where things started to go wrong.

It wasn't Chicopee's fault. Chicopee, like Auburn, was nothing but a gathering place, a town with easy access to the Mass Pike and a parking lot where bus trippers could leave their cars for a couple of days. And for all I know, the troop of drunken stumble-bums who boarded the bus at Chicopee had driven in from Springfield, Agawam, Westfield, or Northampton. But it's still hard to resist blaming Chicopee. It's hard not to think about how much better our trip might have been if Sid had somehow spaced out as he approached Exit 5 on the Pike and we'd sailed on through the Berkshires and into New York without looking back.

But he didn't. And as we pulled into the industrial site where the Chicopee gang was waiting, I could smell trouble.

There were two groups in the lot, all men. There was a pair of young guys, maybe college students, who stood by their car chatting. And on the other side of a line of vehicles, there was a group of half a dozen. Four of them appeared to be about my age, mid-30s; the other two looked a good bit older, 50ish maybe. They all had the thick fingers and weather-worn faces that I associate with construction workers, and their plaid Woolrich jackets and old down vests, for some reason, made me figure they were more likely framers than finish guys. Of course, they might have been masons, roofers, or landscapers for all I knew. What was certain was that they worked with their hands and they worked outdoors.

None of that was a sign of trouble, though. What was troubling about the guys in the larger Chicopee group was that none them looked particularly fresh. They all wore weary, bleary, bedraggled looks on their faces that said the drinks in their hands weren't meant to start the morning as much as to wipe away the remnants of the night before. Hair of the dog may be a good hangover remedy, but it typically doesn't make for pleasant company.

Still, as the two younger guys found seats toward the middle of the bus and the other six filed past us on their way to the back, I found a way to feel hopeful about the journey and a little bit bad about myself. They probably wouldn't be as much trouble as they looked, I thought. And I was probably exhibiting some kind of shameful elitist snobbery merely by suspecting them. Even if they did turn out to be disruptive drunks, I figured, it wouldn't last. They'd probably closed some bar on Friday night. They'd be exhausted and pass out a couple miles down the road.

That kind of optimism never pays.

It's not that there was nothing enjoyable about the trek across New York. It was good to hang out with Don. And nice that this time around neither of us needed to drive.

Don and I both earn part of our living as music journalists, so we talked about music and work. We played cribbage. Don told me about the greyhounds he and his wife, Kate, had adopted, and about how Kate was spending the weekend with other greyhound enthusiasts. He gave me some background on his friend Keith, at whose house I'd be watching the Pats play the Chicago Bears in a week.

I told Don about the home improvement projects my wife and I had taken on, and about how I'd left her at home to continue those projects while I tripped off to Buffalo.

And Don shared his theory on how the Pats were bound to come out of Buffalo with a win.

Belichick has always had Bledsoe's number, he insisted. The numbers bore him out, too. In Belichick's three years as defensive coordinator with the Jets, New York was 4–2 against the Pats, putting up 155 points to New England's 117. Even during Belichick's mostly unsuccessful tenure as head coach of the old Cleveland Browns, his team had managed to win two out of three matches with the Patriots, including a '94 wild card play-off game that Cleveland took 20–13. In Don's mind, Belichick's success stopping Bledsoe-run offenses and Buffalo's lack of a powerful running game added up to a Patriots win in the making.

I wasn't entirely convinced. As money managers are wont to disclaim, past performance is no guarantee of future success. But it did feel better to have something solid to hang my hopes on.

As bus 11 climbed through the hills, then zipped over the Thruway, the scene in the back grew progressively more repulsive.

It started out with plain old loudness, with drunks being drunks, swearing at each other, belching at each other, and announcing their drinking successes to the rest of us (who failed, I'm afraid, to provide the attention they were seeking).

By the time we got to Albany, it had escalated to ugly loudness. Nothing special, mind you, just the usual belligerent moron babble—You ready for another beer? No? What are you, a girl? What are you, a fag? (And if you're a fag, do you know Drew Bledsoe? Because apparently he's a fag, too.) How'd you get your wife to let you off the leash? Fuckin' Bills *suck!*—unclever, unsubstantial, and always laced with fear and anger.

By Utica, the fellas had added farting to the program. Maybe not all of them, but more than one. Beer farts. Some loud enough to get the other jackasses laughing. Some made known to those of us in their paths only by the hooting and hollering coming from the back of the bus. And one of those fuckheads produced a stream of farts that managed to turn his friends' stomachs as easily as the rest of ours.

The rest of us did nothing. We rolled our eyes at each other. We concentrated on our own conversations. We paid attention to whatever movie was playing on the little TV screens (*Lord of the Rings,* I think, and maybe *The Rookie*). And we waited for Joe to deal with the problem. But he never did.

It never got any louder or any uglier. It just never got any quieter or less hateful. And the fact that it didn't get better made it worse.

Things got better when we got off the bus.

The tour company booked us into the team hotel, which was really more exciting to Don than it was to me. But it felt like something special just the same. Having a drink in the lobby bar, we spotted players milling about on the mezzanine. We guessed one of them was Roman Pfifer and another one was Tebucky Jones, but it's hard to know these guys without their numbers.

Someone reported seeing Ty Law in an elevator and Don kiddingly instructed, "The players are coursing among us. Write that. They're coursing among us."

While waiting for a table in a brew pub near the hotel, we watched Boston College end Notre Dame's shot at topping the college football polls. We met a couple of Pats fans who had come in from DC for the game. We drank a couple of average microbrews and ate a heavy, cheese-drenched dinner.

And we ended the night back in the hotel bar, talking to a big Bledsoe fan from Dracut, Massachusetts, and listening to an older guy at the bar's piano play the Notre Dame fight song as if it were a dirge.

Bus 11 was one man light the next morning. One of the Chicopee crew, surprisingly, got into a fight and was arrested. I'm sure everyone on the bus mourned his absence.

Sid had to make a speech, indirectly directed to the idiot squad, about keeping the bus clean and using the bathroom properly.

"These are adults, right?" I asked Don. "Adults?"

The bus ride out to Orchard Park was short and blissfully uneventful. And with most of 1,000 people at the travel agency tailgate party, there was no need for us to be anywhere near the back-of-the-bus brigade.

Sitting at a banquet table working my way through a plate of sausage, chicken, and potato salad, I started to feel good about the afternoon ahead. Without reason, and without any direct prompting, I started to believe the Pats could win the game. I thought about saying so, but I decided I didn't trust the feeling. I figured I was just feeling the effects of 30 hours spent surrounded by Patriots fans. I figured I was probably wrong.

Don and I went into Ralph Wilson Stadium early. We walked down to the lowest level of the stands and watched the Patriots warm up.

The size of a professional football player strikes you when you're that close up. You realize, seeing these guys on TV or at a distance, that they're giants, but standing nearby them, you can actually see how much bigger they are than any average person. It's intimidating and impressive.

As we climbed up to section 332, we talked about how Ralph Wilson Stadium has the same design as the Patriots' old home. It's a piece of shit. The cramped bathrooms with their trough urinals, the concrete stands that look like they're on the verge of collapse, the narrow, claustrophobic passageways and tiny concession windows—all reminders of how awful things used to be.

There was nothing at all awful about the game. The Patriots scored on their first possession, held the Bills to 48 yards of total offense in the first quarter, then scored again to start the second quarter. Both Patriots touchdowns came in the air.

The Pats led 17–7 at halftime. By the end of the third quarter, running backs Kevin Faulk and Antowain Smith had added a touchdown apiece. The defense, meanwhile, had kept the Bills from improving their score. Bledsoe had completed only about two-thirds of his passes. He'd taken a few sacks. And he was getting virtually no help from running backs Travis Henry and Larry Centers.

Midway through the fourth quarter, Brady put up his third touchdown pass of the day, a nice little screen right that Antowain Smith advanced 14 yards for the score. Two plays later, Bledsoe threw an interception.

There's been plenty of awful stuff going on in section 332, though. And now it's reached a pitch.

A pair of the delightful chaps from the back of our bus have the seats directly to my left. They were drunk coming into the stadium and they've grown steadily more inebriated through the game.

One of them, the one who looks like a thinner, harder, more battle-scarred Barney Gumble, is quickly approaching comatose (he was merely stupefied when he and his buddy arrived shortly after kickoff). He's spent much of the game staring at midfield, reacting to almost nothing that's happened except when prodded by his friend. He's snapped back to consciousness every once in a long while, but only long enough to attempt another sip of his beer. And at those moments he's typically managed to dump more of his flat brew on my leg ("Oh, uh, sorry") than he's got in his mouth.

The other has been staggering along the line between obnoxious and belligerent. He wears a ragged goatee on a face that seems made for mug shots. And his drunken grin reveals a chipped front tooth that I'd lay solid odds speaks to a history of bar fights.

He's been looking for a fight with two or three rows of Bills fans seated behind us since the Pats scored their first touchdown, turning to taunt them (sloppily—a drunken "Hah" and a finger point most often) at every opportunity and adopting a "Who, me?" attitude—shrugging, palms raised—when someone shouts at him to sit his ass back down.

If I hadn't already developed an intense hatred for them on the bus, though, those two might have been easy for me to write off. They were, after all, just a couple of standard-issue yahoos making asses of themselves. There would just have been the matter of Don and I disassociating ourselves from them. And we accomplished that during their second-quarter trip to the beer stands, informing the increasingly annoyed Bills fans nearby that the jackasses were not actually with us. We even attempted to convince the home crowd that we were more typical of Pats fans than the drunks.

Trouble is, there are thousands and thousands of Patriots fans at Ralph Wilson Stadium today and most of them are almost as bad as the boys from the back of the bus.

I don't know whether the bulk of the Pats fans who attended the game were as drunk as my neighbors. I can't imagine they were. It doesn't matter. Drunkenness may or may not be a part of the problem, but it's not any excuse.

Watching your team win on someone else's field, you have to know the difference between celebrating and taunting. You're allowed to be excited. You're allowed to cheer. You're allowed to jump and dance, high-five and hug. You can hoot and whistle. You can express your pride in your team. But you can't be ungracious; you can't turn to the people next to you watching their team take a beating and tell them they suck. You can't jeer them as they head for the gates. You can't act like some kind of savage.

Only what I should say about engaging in awful behavior isn't that you can't but that you shouldn't. Because you can. And, unfortunately for all of us, much of the giant group of Pats fans here in the back of the stadium does.

After Bledsoe throws the pick, a lot of the Bills fans decide to get heading home. Now the Pats fans own the stadium and they break into song: "Na na na na, na na na na, hey hey hey, goo-ood-bye."

That's fine. It isn't exactly imaginative, but it's fine. It's a football game, after all. And it's the first time Pats fans have seen a win since September 22.

But then the song ends before the gang in the back has had enough—so they try something else, something they've stolen from the Jets.

"P-A-T-S, Pats, Pats, Pats!" they chant.

I turn to Don, and he's got the same pained expression on his face as I do.

"Oh, God," I say. "They didn't really do that, right?"

They do it again before Don has a chance to answer. And I sink down as far as I can in my seat. They've officially made it difficult to feel good about what's happening on the field.

The problem isn't simply that they've adapted the Jets cheer. Under the right circumstances (specifically, a rout of the Jets in front of their famously obnoxious fans), that would be cool, even funny. But these aren't the right circumstances. What's happening here is that a bunch of rowdies whose distinctly unproven team has been good enough and lucky enough to beat a strong division rival have gotten their chests puffed out and their heads swollen. And now they're berating the home team and its fans, who have been nothing but gracious hosts (except, maybe, to the guy who got arrested, and I'm just guessing he wasn't everything Buffalo was looking for in a tourist). In short, the Pats fans here aren't simply sounding like Jets fans, they're behaving like Jets fans.

Then comes another chant, a lilting taunt of "Blehhhhhd-soooooe, Blehhhhhd-soooooe, Blehhhhhd-soooooe." It starts in the far end zone and works its way around. And although it's sort of expected, and although I'm sure Bledsoe can handle it, it's still unbecoming. After all, it's not like Bledsoe ditched the Patriots; the Patriots ditched him.

A minute later that P-A-T-S taunt reemerges. And while I'm determined to see this game to the very end, I start glancing around at the exits.

Happiness takes over again as soon as we get some distance from section 332. As we walk across the street, even as we search endlessly for bus 11 among a sea of others (they all look the same), what's most on my mind is the Patriots' win.

The Pats have won a game they couldn't afford to lose. They've beaten a team they had to beat if they hope to contend for the AFC East title. They've evened up their record with a big win on the road. And they've done it all by playing good, solid football. The fact that they ran all over a team with a suspect defense isn't impressive all by itself. But the fact that they stopped a team with a powerhouse offense is—even if it's true that Belichick has Bledsoe's number.

It'll take a win next week at Chicago (probably much more) before I'm ready even to start thinking of truly believing in the Pats again, but 38–7 is at least enough to make me feel glad to have taken the trip.

I haven't forgotten the jerks at the back of section 332 ("You can't go around acting like Jets fans," I say to Don out of the clear blue at one point), but I know I'll never have to see most of them again, which is comforting.

I haven't forgotten the guys in the back of the bus either. There are still five out of six assholes who will almost certainly find a way to make the ride home even less pleasant than the ride to Buffalo. Sitting back in the bus listening to the angry Buffalo sports talkers on the radio, I try to prepare for the return of the all-yahoo team. They'll be drunk. They'll be charged up. They'll be at full power.

And, of course, they are all of those things. They enter the bus loudly, with drunken smirks on their faces. They settle into their seats with much commotion. And they begin bickering and taunting each other. "Nice pants, you fucking queer," one shouts to another in the course of some debate about nothing. Terrific.

I can't hear the radio anymore. Or I can, but only during the short stretches between outbursts. Don, who has one of the late games on his headset radio, is giving me score updates, though, so I've at least got that.

And when the bus starts out of the parking lot, Joe sticks some awful Tim Allen movie in the VCR, cranking up the volume just enough so that I can kind of block out the idiocy drifting forward on tufts of flatulence.

I think, 38–7. That's what's important.

It's true. The win is the most important thing to come out of this day. The embarrassment I felt in the stands will fade. The anger I'm feeling toward the jerks in the back (and toward Joe for failing to do anything about it) will abate. But the hash mark in the Patriots win column will endure through the season.

And in those odd moments when the back of the bus actually approaches silence, I can usually get my head around the outcome of the game well enough to keep myself happy.

9.

Game 9 at Chicago Bears

Sunday, November 10, 2002
Record 4–4

One second everyone's chanting—"It's o-ver! It's o-ver!"—the next they're scrambling.

The big TV has gone black just as the refs are about tell us whether the Patriots–Chicago Bears game is, in fact, all but over. The connection has gone dead, with the exquisite, painful, seemingly sentient timing of cable TV.

The replay official has been reviewing a call on the field, attempting to make sure that David Patten really did get both feet inbounds on a 20-yard touchdown pass. If the score stands, it will put the Patriots ahead by one point with 21 seconds remaining in the game. If the call on the field is overturned, the Pats will face fourth and three. They'll be five points back, 20 yards out, and one broken play away from their fifth loss of the season.

The nine of us gathered around a big old cabinet-style Zenith television in the corner of a partially finished basement in New Boston, New Hampshire, already know how the review ought to turn out. CBS has shown the replay several times. There's no doubt about it: Patten got his right foot down solidly, then managed to drag his left foot as he teetered out of the back of the end zone. That's a touchdown. It's o-ver!

But it's not like replay reviews never go the wrong way. And it's not like fans don't see things the way they want them to be. So it's not unthinkable that the Pats could end up being stripped of the touchdown. There's always a chance that the ref walks back on the field and says Patten never got that left foot down. And after that kind of letdown, the game might soon be o-ver the wrong way.

We're excited. We're tense. The energy built up over the course of a big fourth quarter comeback by the Pats began exploding into the room with Patten's athletic catch. But the charge has been frozen, held in stasis by a guy in a black-and-white striped shirt, since shortly thereafter. And you can feel it hanging in the air, ready to jump back to life—or drop straight down to the floor. I've been just about doubled over in my seat, hands clasped behind my head, forearms tight against my temples, elbows just about touching my knees. Others have been leaning in toward the TV. A couple of guys have stayed on their feet since the initial call. One's been bouncing on his toes a bit. The other has stood dead still. Fists have been clenched in hope. One pair of eyes has been closed.

When the picture disappears, we spend a few stunned seconds trying to figure out what happened. Then we start to panic.

Keith, our host, is on top of it, though. He rushes to the smaller TV, the 13-inch set we'd used earlier in the day to stay on top of the Pittsburgh Steelers–Atlanta Falcons game, flips it on, changes the channel, and adjusts the rabbit ears until we get a rough, snowy picture.

The Patriots are back on the field lining up to try a two-point conversion. And though we've missed the replay official's announcement, the fact that the game is progressing this way means he's upheld Patten's touchdown. There's an excited cheer before we snap to silence again, freezing that energy for just another second or two, waiting to celebrate the Pats' win until it's just a little closer to certain.

The Patriots are now up 31–30. The conversion attempt is about bumping their lead to three points. If they pull it off, the Bears won't be able to win at the end of regulation with a field goal.

This is a big deal. It's tough to score a touchdown in 21 seconds, but it's anything but unheard-of for a team to steal a long field goal with that kind of time. And teams win in the closing seconds of NFL games all the time.

The guys gathered here at Keith's house have been as unfalteringly confident in their team as any Patriots fans I've ever seen, believing even through the darkest periods of an extremely difficult game. But there's no such thing as a professional football fan who doesn't know that games this close are never over until the clock ticks down to 00:00.

The Pats make the conversion with a little toss from Tom Brady to Troy Brown. And now the defense will need to protect a lead for the first time all day. They'll need to stop the Bears from using their 21 seconds to pull off a shocker. It looks good. Chicago might manage three points in that little time if they're lucky. But it's pretty obvious that the Pats would win in overtime. It looks like it really is o-ver.

Now that suspended energy finally surges back into motion. It charges outward, bounces off the concrete walls, and doubles back over us. And all at once, eight 30-something men commence a dancing, hugging, high-fiving, laughing, and yelling celebration that most of the sports world is better off for not having witnessed.

All I can do is sit gape-jawed, awed by the Pats' impressive comeback—they had trailed the Bears 27–6 a little more than halfway through the third quarter—a little scared by the celebration happening around me (part of me wishes my wife were here, just so she could see that other guys do victory dances as goofy as my own) and cautiously mindful of the fact that there are still those 21 seconds to play.

Keith emerges from the celebration, giant grin dominating his flushed, round face. He takes a step toward me, bends down just enough to make it clear he's addressing me, laughs, and says, "I think they're fucked." My words from earlier in the quarter, when things looked a good bit less rosy for the Pats.

As usual, I'm the last person in the room to start believing in the Pats (in fact, I'm still 21 seconds away from it); as usual, I've expressed this (though this time only because I was asked); and, as usual, it's coming back at me.

I'm okay with that.

I've been here in the basement for better than four hours now, which has been plenty long enough to learn that Keith and his buddies are a good-natured lot. I can take a little playful ribbing from this kind of crowd, especially considering how great it is to have been wrong.

I know myself. I know how I can be. I've been a pessimist for as long as I can remember. And I certainly have my curmudgeonly qualities. But I'm no crank. I take no pleasure when one of my dark prognostications turns out to be on the mark. And I suffer no displeasure when some dire prediction comes up wrong.

I couldn't be more delighted about the fact that the Patriots are, in fact, not fucked at all. I couldn't be happier when, 21 seconds and three plays after the two-point conversion, the Pats walk off the field in Champaign, Illinois (the Bears' temporary home), with their second consecutive road victory.

Yeah, it took a lot of work to get today's win. Yeah, there have been some troublesome aspects to this game (like the fact that Bears running back Anthony Thomas put up more than 100 yards). And, yeah, the victory comes over a Bears team that has now dropped seven straight. The thing is, none of that stuff matters. All that does matter is this: When the Pats left Foxborough for a three-game road swing eight days ago, they had a losing record. They were not looking like defending champions. They were looking like a run-of-the-mill team that had made at least one horribly misguided personnel move. Two games later, though, they've made a statement about their choice of quarterbacks and they've climbed back up over .500, if only just.

It would be impossible not to feel good about such developments, impossible even for a guy who started the day half expecting the absolute worst.

During my drive up from Northampton to New Boston early in the afternoon, I was actually more inclined to pay attention to the day and the season than to think about football.

Indian summer had set in, allowing me one more chance to drive with the windows down. But the day wasn't nearly so pretty as it was warm. The sky was a silent, muscular gray. And the air was moist and far too heavy for fall. It was March air, not November air.

Passing through the mostly wooded terrain of north-central Massachusetts and the Monadnock Region of southwestern New Hampshire, I watched the way the mustards, burnt oranges, and deep reds were giving way to rich browns and pale yellows. And I thought about how there's a particular romance about this time of year, the border time between the leaf-peeping and skiing seasons. This is the time when you can see the real soul of New England, solemn, stern, and ungenerous, and all the more beautiful for it.

There was, I realized, a connection between my love for this time of year, for days like this one, and my approach to football.

The 2002 season was looking very much like one whose charms were behind it for me. The Patriots were coming off a big win in Buffalo, yes, but they were still at 4–4 on the season. And they still had today's game and a matchup with the Raiders to play before they'd get back to Foxborough. Winning on the road isn't easy in the NFL. So 4–6 was looming as a possibility.

My Raiders, meanwhile, had also dropped to 4–4. They'd started their season with four straight wins, followed by four losses. And they were on their way to face their arch rivals, the 6–2 Denver Broncos, on Monday night.

It was entirely possible that both the Pats and the Raiders would win their games this weekend, but what then? A week later they'd square off against each other, and one of my two favorite teams would be back down to .500 just as the football season began to turn all brown and yellow.

Neither the Pats nor the Raiders really ought to have been in such a difficult position. Both of them had lost games they should have found ways to win. Both of them should have been better than 4–4. And in light of that, I was having a hard time working up any amount of hope for either team.

I've always found it difficult to feel warm toward a team that fails to live up to its potential. It's more pleasing, in many ways, to support a bad team that exceeds your expectations than a good one that disappoints.

Looking out into the granite toughness of the day, that manner of thinking started to make sense. You simply can't expect someone raised by this mother to offer affection easily.

Keith isn't like me. He remains enthusiastic about the Pats in spite of everything that's gone wrong with their season. And he's got more reason to be jaded and stingy with his affections than most sports fans.

I don't really know Keith. He's Don's friend. We played in the same online fantasy football league a few years ago, a league Don organized, and we've spoken on the phone a few times. But we've never actually met before today.

Our backgrounds aren't so different, though. We're about the same age. He grew up in Medway, Massachusetts, a town that borders my hometown of Milford. He worked as a sports stringer for the *Milford Daily News* at a time when I was a young reporter on staff there. And we both left the area at about the same time.

We also both grew up with the same Patriots team. But while I rejected that team, Keith embraced it. He continues to do so. And he continues to maintain the wide-eyed dedication of a true believer despite the fact that he makes his living in the sports world.

A former editor of the collectibles magazine *Tuff Stuff,* Keith currently works for Pacific Trading Cards, a manufacturer of hockey and football cards.

Pacific isn't the biggest name in the sports trading-card world— where Upper Deck and Topps are McDonald's and Burger King— but the company has carved out a nice piece of the football and hockey card market. Pacific manufactures 10 of the 60 lines of football cards on the market. Keith's job is to promote the company's higher-end lines.

Never having had much interest in sports cards, or collectibles of any sort, I needed Keith to describe his world for me.

There are two basic categories of sports cards, he explained. There's retail, the low-end variety of cards, the ones you can buy at the discount department stores and corner drugstores. Those cards are priced to move. Then there's hobby, higher-end cards that you have to go to a specialty shop to buy. They sell for between $3 and $20 a pack.

The cards Keith promotes range from those that are simply constructed better than the drugstore variety up to packs that include such memorabilia items as jersey cards, which have pieces of a real game jerseys (worn by real players), bound into them.

Looking over the array of sample items in Keith's home office, I started to understand how it is that sports trading cards have become a multimillion-dollar industry. The cards Keith sells aren't like the ones we all flipped in the school yard growing up; they're firm, substantial, shiny, pretty. And they're more than that. They offer collectors a chance to connect with sports teams and idols in a manner more tangible than by watching a game. They also offer the fans the opportunity to channel their energy in ways that aren't tied to the fortunes of any team. A collector can win even when his favorite team is losing. He can remain absorbed with his favorite sport even during the off-season.

Even as someone who isn't interested in collectibles, I couldn't miss the fact that Keith has something of a dream job for a sports nut. A lot of what he does involves creating events for hobby-card dealers. He travels to cities across the country and hobnobs with the kind of people who always have tickets to see their home teams. That means Keith gets to go to a lot of pro sports events. And because his company needs him to conduct events for card collectors around football and hockey's biggest games, he gets to go to the Super Bowl every year. There's no way not to envy him for that.

Of course, there's a danger involved in turning something you love into the way you make your living.

To begin with, there are the practical concerns. It's one thing to get excited about a team or a game, to collect cards, autographed photos, and jerseys. It's quite another to tie your mortgage payment, your ability to eat, or your child's future to the hope that other people will share your passion. And even when doing so works out, there's no way to know if it's permanent. America is a nation of trend chasers. A company that's prosperous today can be bankrupt next month.

There's also the risk that the thing you so enjoy will become nothing more than your job.

I've run up against that a number of times as a journalist. Writing about music, sports, and entertainment, I sometimes forget why I got into this line of work in the first place. I can start to think about how I *have* to listen to a CD or watch a game, instead of remembering how amazing it is that I get paid to do things the people around me pay good money to do. I can also forget how to separate listening or watching as a professional and doing so just as a fan. And that can make the simple act of hearing and enjoying a record difficult to pull off.

For a guy like Keith, who is constantly taking in games as a function of his job, the risks are that going to a game will become such a common experience that it's no longer exciting, or, worse still, that watching sports will become so indistinguishable from working that it's no longer fun.

Keith has experienced a little bit of that. He confesses skipping Super Bowl XXXV (in which the Baltimore Ravens beat the New York Giants). He blew that game off in part because he'd had enough of Giants fans after two weeks of trading-card events, and in part because he just wanted to get home.

But Keith's work hasn't affected his lifelong passion for the Patriots. He can't explain that. He can't say why he's able to watch the entire Pats game without once mentioning work; or why, having seen innumerable games, he still gets nervous and excited every game day. It's just working out for him. And he's not about to pick that apart.

There's been a steady stream of food—chicken, sausage, ribs, shrimp, pizza—since I arrived at three o'clock. There have been darts matches. There's been an almost continuous round of this game Keith invented involving a ring, a piece of string, and some hooks screwed into a two-by-four that hangs from one of the ceiling joists: you're supposed to swing the ring and hook the hooks in a particular order. And there have been Strat-O-Matic baseball matchups playing out all over the basement since I arrived. It's opening weekend in Keith's Strat-O-Matic Old-Timers league.

Strat-O-Matic is the Dungeons & Dragons of the fantasy-sports universe—with a lot more yelling and a lot less pewter. Sports geeks gather in basements all over America with statistical charts for their teams (usually current teams, but in this case it's classic squads, mostly World Series contenders, like the '67 Red Sox and '54 Indians) and play games based on strategies too complicated to absorb in a single afternoon, and executed by rolling dice and interpreting the rolls against team stats.

I don't play Strat-O-Matic. It's a bit too involved for me. But as someone who maintains two fantasy football teams and takes the competition in my fantasy leagues a bit more seriously than is healthy, I get the instinct.

This day was never really about Strat-O-Matic baseball, though. Nor darts, nor rings on strings. It was always about the Patriots-Bears game. And that part hasn't always been fun.

The game started slow. Neither team managed to score in the first quarter. They traded field goals in the second, with Adam Vinatieri and Bears kicker Paul Edinger putting up six points apiece.

Things started to go wrong early in the second half. The Patriots' first possession ended after just two plays as Brady took a hit and lost the ball. Chicago took over at the Patriots' 14 yard line and scored two plays later.

On their next possession, the Pats went three and out. The Bears scored a 44-yard touchdown on their first play after the punt. Chicago looked like they were breaking it open.

Halfway through the quarter, Brady was picked off by linebacker Brian Urlacher at the Pats' 36 yard line. Three plays later, Thomas found the end zone.

The Pats were down three touchdowns and Brady was looking like he'd forgotten how to hold on to the ball.

Keith and his pals grew sour—when Phil Simms, who was in the booth for CBS, noted that the Pats needed to take the rest of their day "one first down at a time," Keith snapped, "How about that philosophy?"—but they never gave up hope.

The Pats put up a 15-yard touchdown pass with six and a half minutes to play in the third and Keith said, "That's it. They can do this." It didn't matter to him that the Pats were trailing by 14, one more point than they'd scored all day. He believed.

"This is a winnable game," one of the crowd (the guy they called Westy, I think) opined after Vinatieri added his third field goal of the day toward the end of the period. No one argued.

If it had been an old friend rather than a new acquaintance making such a statement, I'd have scoffed. But it wasn't. So I didn't. Why be a wet blanket?

Even absent verbalization, though, Keith had a good sense of my skepticism. He and I had discussed my feelings about the Pats on the phone earlier in the week. He was aware of how reluctant I am to jump on the bandwagon even at the brightest moments. He had to know I wasn't on board just then.

So I happily dropped my reluctance to speak when Keith invited my negativity into the conversation midway through the fourth quarter.

The Bears, leading by eight following a Vinatieri field goal, lined up at the Pats' 16 yard line, then committed a holding penalty on a third-down play that ended in an incompletion.

Bill Belichick had a choice: take the penalty, which would have backed Chicago up to the 26 but given them another shot at third down, or let the play stand, leaving Chicago to face fourth down but giving Edinger an easy 23-yard chip shot. He opted for the chip shot and the Bears went ahead 30–19.

The guys divided over whether Belichick had made the right call on the penalty. I simply sat back, taking it in, assuming it didn't much matter (assuming, that is, that the Pats weren't going to make up eight points, let alone 11). But Keith sucked me into it. "What do you think?" he asked.

I said what popped into my head: "I think they're fucked."

It took less than four minutes of game time for those words to begin coming back at me.

After the Pats scored on a 36-yard touchdown pass from Brady to Kevin Faulk with 2:46 remaining in the game, closing the gap to five points, Keith looked at me sideways and whispered the sentence back to me: "I think they're fucked." An odd, inexplicable confidence that his team was anything but fucked shone out of his eyes. I thought about pointing out that the Pats had just missed a key two-point conversion (which would have brought them to within a field goal), but there was something about Keith's faith in his team that stopped me.

The Pats D stopped Chicago, giving Brady and the offense the ball back at the two-minute warning.

The Pats pushed to the Bears' 30 yard line. Then defensive end Bryan Robinson intercepted a Brady pass. Robinson dropped the ball during the interception return, but his teammate, tackle Roosevelt Colvin, covered it up.

That would have ended the game, but the refs reviewed the call in replay and overturned the ruling on the field, saying Robinson never had complete possession. That made it an incomplete pass, giving the Pats one more chance. When the replay ruling was announced, as his friends jumped around hooting, Keith glanced at me, saying nothing but thinking it hard enough that I could feel it: "I think they're fucked."

And now, with 21 seconds to play and the outcome all but certain, there's no reason Keith shouldn't just come right out and say it. He's earned it—and so have I.

"I guess they're not fucked," I admit.

Keith laughs, then gets back to celebrating with his buddies.

We watch on the little TV—with the horizontal hold failing, dumping a bar right through the middle of the screen—as the Bears fail to make anything of their last possession. Then with the final seconds ticking off the game clock, guys start getting ready to leave. It's getting late—20 minutes to eight o'clock—and most of us have long drives home ahead of us. New Boston isn't close to anything.

I thank Keith for inviting me into his home, then head for the door. And then something strikes me.

"Seems like the kind of comeback that can turn a whole season around," I say, hardly believing the words are coming out of my mouth.

"You're right," Keith answers. "It does."

But I'm still a Raiders fan first. And the Pats travel to Oakland next. So I'm hoping New England doesn't turn its season around too quickly.

I also remain as committed a skeptic as Keith is a fan. So as I walk down the long, dark driveway under a starless sky, I can't help but wonder if those words won't come back to haunt me, too.

10.

Game 10 at Oakland Raiders

Sunday, November 17, 2002
Record 5–4

There's a steady clinking and an occasional pounding from the booth behind me. Two waitresses are combining the contents of half-empty ketchup bottles. Business is pretty slow tonight at Rafters pub in Amherst. The waitresses need something to do.

There's the waitresses' conversation, too. They're discussing an upcoming wedding. I'm not sure whose. One of the waitresses is supposed to be in the wedding, but she doesn't want to be. The other one isn't even invited, though she seems to know the bride fairly well. Still, she doesn't seem too broken up about not being on the guest list. But I'm not listening. Or anyhow, I'm trying not to listen. I don't really want to listen.

There are the sounds of the foursome at the booth behind my wife. They're conversing in Japanese, laughing, and loudly sucking buffalo sauce from their fingers—a steady sequence of long, greasy finger sucks that make us wince and make me wonder whatever happened to manners.

From the far side of the bar, way over across the room, there are the muffled sounds of conversation, occasionally cut with laughter but largely flat, dispassionate.

There's been grumbling in various spots from time to time throughout the night, but not now. There's been a cheer here or there, but not lately. Mostly, there's a quiet hanging over the place, a thicker, more oppressive version of the general hush that's been on this pub since we walked in at 6:30.

* * *

I've wondered at times throughout the night if the mood was perhaps a result of the weather. It's been raining or snowing (often both) for two days now; Maybe it's just gotten to people.

There's something rotten and wholly depressing about getting winter weather this early on. Forget that it won't technically be winter for another month, we haven't even hit Thanksgiving yet. And romantic fantasies about sleigh rides to Grandmother's house don't do a thing to lift your spirits when you're rooting through the tool shed, searching for your snow shovel in the middle of November.

The weather has certainly contributed to the sparseness of the crowd at Rafters tonight. The pub, which sits less than a mile from the University of Massachusetts, Amherst, campus is typically packed on the night of a big game. Locals and students jam the big bar area and the dining room alike. But not tonight. The place has approached full at points, but there have never been more people here than there are chairs and bar stools. Almost no one wants to leave their house on a night like this.

It doesn't strike me as going too far out on a limb to guess that the weather is at least partially responsible for the glum spirit that's been holding on at Rafters since well before the start of the Patriots' Sunday night game against the Oakland Raiders.

I can't help thinking there was always something more to it, though. I keep thinking the mood here has been tied to the weird vibe I'd felt all day, the one that said the Patriots were headed for a loss.

I didn't put too much stock in that vibe during the day. I'm not the kind of person who's given to trusting in odd premonitions. Too spooky. I'm always ready to make predictions about the outcome of games, but I never base them solely on gut. I need to look at the stats and the trends, consider the injury reports, and look at the weather forecast. It's not an exact science, but it's a science just the same. And science has to be more reliable than psychic vibrations.

So I'd just written the vibe off as a manifestation of my ambivalence about tonight's game, which has pitted my chosen team, the Raiders, against the home team I've always been reluctantly fond of. But maybe I was wrong. Maybe there really was something more than freezing rain and wet snow in the air. Maybe the others felt it too, and maybe it meant something to them.

There's only one situation in which I ever root against the Patriots and tonight's game is it.

It's not easy. I'd be much happier if the Raiders and Pats were in different conferences. Then I'd only have to take sides against New England once every four years—and maybe, if the stars were ever to line up in just exactly the most difficult way, in a Super Bowl. But I'm not that lucky. I have to face one of these days at least every couple of years.

Tonight it's been more difficult than usual to back the Patriots' opponents. For one thing, even though the time I've spent watching the Pats and hanging out with fans hasn't turned me into a faithful believer, it has made me more of a Pats fan than I've ever been. For another, the Pats took the field in Oakland very much in need of a win. They came into this weekend in a three-way tie for the lead in the AFC East. The Pats, the Bills, and the Dolphins all stood at 5–4 going into today. The Jets were one game out at 4–5. By the time Sunday night came around, though, the other teams in the division had wrapped up their matches. The Dolphins hammered the Baltimore Colts 26–7. The Jets took advantage of the Detroit Lions 31–14. And the Bills lost a close one to the Kansas City Chiefs 17–16. So a Pats win would keep them in a first-place tie with the Fins, while a loss would knock them into a three-way tie for second with the other teams.

But I'm still a Raiders fan first. And the Raiders need the win tonight even more than the Patriots.

Oakland snapped a four-game losing streak and improved to 5–4 with a huge win over the Denver Broncos on Monday night. But they still trail the 6–3 Broncos and the 6–3 San Diego Chargers in the AFC West. And the Broncos and Chargers both won their week 11 games, which meant the Raiders would need to win just to remain a game back.

In all honesty, though, my feelings about this game probably would have been no less mixed even if the Raiders had come in at 9–0, solidly in command of their division, and able to give up a loss without worry. I'm not like my buddy Tom, who backed the Pats against his Broncos because he thought the local squad needed a win more. I always want the Raiders to win. But I almost always want the Patriots to win, too, these days nearly as much.

There are situations in which I could root for the Pats against the Raiders happily and without reservation. If it were the last game of the season, the Raiders were 2–13 and the Pats needed a win to make the play-offs, I'd surely support the Pats. I'd assuage my feelings about betraying Oakland by telling myself that a loss would actually be best for the Raiders, preserving, and perhaps improving, their position in the order for the next year's draft. I still wouldn't be able to resist getting excited if the Raiders came into such a game and flattened the Pats (I like watching my team play well), but I'd feel bad about feeling good.

The circumstances of tonight's game haven't been nearly so simple, though. And even if they were, there's something else. There's a little matter of revenge.

The Pats are due a bit of payback for what took place when these two teams met in that snowy divisional play-off game 10 months ago. Pats fans call it the tuck game. Raiders fans call it the snow job. The long and short of it is that the Pats got the better part of a bad piece of officiating. And the lucky break that moved the Pats along on the path to victory in Super Bowl XXXVI was the unlucky break that sent the Raiders home empty-handed.

I have a certain amount of ambivalence even there, though. Bad calls happen. You have to overcome them. And the fact that the Raiders didn't end up winning that game in overtime indicates they didn't deserve to win. So I have to concede that the better team came out ahead even if it did need a little help getting there. Plus, maybe the Raiders would have lost to Pittsburgh. Or to St. Louis.

Then there's the fact that Super Bowl XXXVI was one of the greatest championship games in league history. And the fact that there's probably never been a more honorable and respectable bunch of professional football players than the 2001 New England Patriots. With the exception of wide receiver Terry Glenn, who hardly played all season (due to a minor injury and a major attitude problem) and wasn't really part of the team, that Pats squad was devoid of players with pro sports egos. It was filled with competitive young men, each of whom recognized that he needed his teammates and that he fared best when he put the team ahead of himself. It was the team whose members declined to be introduced individually at the Super Bowl, coming out onto the field as a unit. The Patriots championship wasn't just good for New England. It was good for professional football. It was good for all of professional sports. So part of me, however small a part it might be, is glad the Pats caught a break in that play-off game.

That said, last season isn't this season. That game wasn't this game. And payback was still on the menu.

The feeling I carried around with me all day wasn't about payback, though. It was never the feeling that the Raiders were going to win. That kind of vibe, in spite of all my ambivalence, would have made me excited, energetic, sunny.

A real Raiders win—a crushing Raiders win—likewise would have wiped away my mixed emotions, replacing them with unapologetic pride and enthusiasm.

But I didn't get a Raiders win. What I got was a Patriots loss. A pitiful, inept, stumbling Patriots loss.

That's precisely what I'd felt coming, too. It was a Pats loss that was hanging in the cold, wet, uncomfortable air today. It's depressing to think about. And as I listen to the waitresses talking, the finger suckers sucking, and the two dozen or so Pats fans who are still here failing to respond to the game, it occurs to me that others must have felt the Patriots' loss in the air, too. They must have, because they don't seem at all surprised to have witnessed it.

Things might have worked out differently if I had been able to find a place to watch the game with other Raiders fans.

I tried. For months, in fact. I asked everyone I know who goes out to bars to watch football games if they'd ever come across a place in New England where Raiders fans gather. I would have driven to Burlington, Maine, to Bangor, Maine, even, if I could have found a place.

I asked the only other Raiders fans I talk to regularly: an old friend who lives here in Amherst and the guy who delivers mail to my office. I asked random New England–based Raiders fans I found on the Internet. They all said they watch games at home on their couches. Like me. Sometimes, a few of them said, they go to some local bar where they're usually the only Raiders fan in the crowd. Like me.

I found a list of Raiders booster clubs online. The closest one to New England is in Westchester County, New York. The president has no listed e-mail address and the phone number given on the Web site doesn't work.

I called some guy in Brookline because he was on the membership roster of something called the Oakland Raiders Internet Boosters. He couldn't help. And I'm pretty sure the call just kind of freaked him out.

I turned to the team, phoning their press office to ask if they were aware of any regional gathering spot for silver-and-black faithful. The woman who took my call could only laugh. "You're a Raiders fan in New England?" she said. "I'm pretty sure that's illegal."

She gave me the name of the guy in Westchester County, thinking maybe he'd know something. She also gave me the same phone number I got off the Web. I didn't bother to tell her I'd already tried him.

There was a hint, late in the week, that I might be able to find a few other Raiders fans in a bar in Milford, Connecticut. If the weather wasn't too bad, a guy told me by e-mail, I might run into two or three Raiders fans in a bar called Gipper's. I actually thought about making the drive, which runs close to two hours in perfect weather. But then winter showed up and I thought better of it.

I took my wife up on her standing offer to accompany me to watch a game if I ever found myself in dire need of a game-day sidekick (an extremely generous offer, given that the woman can't even pretend to enjoy football) and stayed in my neck of the woods.

My wife grabbed a book (which she'd end up reading through the game) and we headed to the sports bar nearest the UMass campus. I figured there had to be a Raiders fan or two on campus, and I hoped one of them would end up making the short drive down the street. By the time we got to Rafters, I really just hoped to find one other person for whom the joy of a Raiders win would offset the pain of a Pats loss. Or, in a worst-case scenario, someone who could share the potential taunting if the Pats somehow pulled off a victory.

Watching the Chargers come back late in their game against San Francisco, I started to think I might have gotten lucky. A group of three young men seated near one of the big-screen TVs was rooting loudly for the 49ers. Maybe, I thought, they were really rooting against the Chargers. Maybe they were Raiders fans in for the night game and hoping the Chargers would drop to 6–4.

I craned my neck trying to get a better look at them in between bites of my Cajun chicken sandwich. I hoped maybe I'd spot a Raiders game jersey. I took an unnecessary trip to the men's room, just so I could pass them, hoping my Raiders sweatshirt would draw some cry of solidarity. Nothing. And then they left almost immediately after the Chargers won in overtime. Niners fans, maybe. Or gamblers. Either way, not what I was hoping for.

I kept an eye on the pub's wooden front door until game time, looking for silver and black with every creak. But all I got was a stream of Pats caps and Tom Brady game jerseys (and a single Tedy Bruschi).

There was a sense of anticipation in the room as game time approached. But it was a dreadful anticipation, an expression of that collective sense that something was amiss.

The crowd lacked any real energy. Most fans couldn't even find it in them to give me a hard time. I heard a hiss at one point as I walked to the men's room. Once inside, though, I ended up in a conversation with some Pats fans about the Raiders running backs. They thought Charlie Garner was overused, Tyrone Wheatley underused, and Zack Crockett overrated. I disagreed with them on the first point, agreed with them on the middle, and opted to reserve judgment on the last.

When I walked over by the bar to check final scores on some four o'clock games 15 minutes before the Pats-Raiders kickoff, a young guy with a mischievous smile said "Raiders fan?" and turned his eyes in mock horror. It made the women he was sitting with laugh. Got a chuckle out of me, too. But it really wasn't anything. Not really.

The mood never truly picked up during the game, either. As the Pats drove down the field without difficulty on their first possession of the game, the crowd was unmoved. They sat in silence as Brady led the offense with completion after completion—four yards to Deion Branch, five to Christian Fauria, another six to Branch—looking like he might actually have it in him to lead his team to a third-straight road victory. No one stood, shouted, or groaned as wide receiver David Givens fumbled at the Oakland 19 yard line. Nor was there a cry of relief when Mike Light recovered the fumble for the Patriots.

I heard a couple of muted expressions of excitement when Vinatieri put up the game's first points, but there was no sense of "Wait a minute, the Pats could win this one" about them.

Once in a while, the Pats fans actually cheered. Like when Raiders quarterback Rich Gannon was sacked deep in Patriots territory early in the second quarter. Once in a while, one or two of them swore out loud. Like three plays after the sack of Gannon, when Crockett bullied his way into the end zone from two yards out. And now and again, one of them would crack a joke. Like when Brady fumbled at the Patriots' nine yard line late in the second quarter and a college kid in a backward baseball cap yelled, "It was a tuck!"

But mostly the Pats fans sat silent. And so did I.

When things went well for the Patriots it was almost as if it were in error.

Linebacker Tedy Bruschi returned an interception 48 yards for a touchdown late in the third quarter, but the play was a fluke. The pass Bruschi caught should have hit the ground and been ruled incomplete, but safety Lawyer Milloy's foot happened to be in the right place at the right time. The ball bounced off Milloy's shoe and into Bruschi's hands. It was exciting for a second in the way strange plays are always exciting. But it wasn't exactly the Immaculate Interception; it only got the Pats to within 11 points (at 24–13). And it failed to energize the team or the fans.

A pair of Brady fumbles that went uncalled by the refs may have angered Raiders fans at the game in Oakland, but they did little to stir the Pats fans in Amherst.

And while the Pats defense held the Raiders without a score through most of the rest of the game, giving up only a 28-yard field goal with just over a minute remaining in the fourth quarter, the New England offense managed nothing throughout the latter part of the game.

The crowd dwindled steadily over the course of the second half. And by the time the Pats turned the ball over on downs late in the game, there were few fans left. Those who remained didn't bother to express any feelings about the incomplete pass on fourth and six that gave the Raiders the ball at the Pats' 43 yard line.

And now it's all but over. Raiders kicker Sebastian Janikowski has made the score 27–13. And the Pats team on the field tonight doesn't have it in them to put up two touchdowns in a minute and 13 seconds.

The ketchup bottles clink along. The finger suckers pay their tab and get up to leave. The few fans still hanging on are more interested in socializing than watching the game.

There's a shallow cheer when Kevin Faulk returns a kickoff 86 yards to make the score 27–20, but no one fools himself into believing the touchdown really means anything. A failed on-side kick attempt and a minute of game time later, it's over. The Raiders have their revenge. And the Pats have a long trip home ahead of them.

The Patriots have a pair of winnable games coming up. They host the underachieving Minnesota Vikings next week. Then they travel to Detroit for what should be an easy victory on Thanksgiving. But there's no such thing as certainty when it comes to this Pats team.

I went into tonight's game thinking the Patriots could probably win five of their last six games, possibly all of them. I thought their wins at Buffalo and Chicago had put them on track to turn their season around, take the AFC East title, and head into the play-offs with some momentum. Now I think I may have been sorely mistaken.

The Raiders, meanwhile, have got their season back on track with their wins against Denver and New England. But I'm not sure it will last. They've got the Arizona Cardinals next week, which is about as close to a guaranteed win as you get in the NFL. Then they head into a series of conference and division games that will decide their season. They'll need to win at least four of their last five to ensure a play-off berth. That won't be easy. They'll need to play a lot better than they played tonight to get there.

As we head back out to my car, a break in the sleet allowing us to walk rather than trying to run across the icy parking lot, my wife notices that I'm uncharacteristically silent.

"Your team won, right?" she says. She knows the answer. She's just trying to figure out what's up with my mood. I should be happy, but I'm not.

I consider explaining that although it's good to have the win, tonight's game hasn't really proven anything about the Raiders. All it's really shown is that the Patriots still haven't solved the identity crisis that's been dogging them throughout this postchampionship season. The Pats still haven't proven they can beat good teams. That's a problem. It's a problem that's started to weigh on my mind—and the minds of all the real Pats fans, too, I think.

But my thoughts about football wouldn't mean anything to my wife. She'd listen politely, as she usually does, but even if she wanted to join in a discussion on the subject she wouldn't know where to start. So I just answer her question.

"Yes, they did," I say.

"So that's good," she offers, hoping to get something out of me.

"Yes," I say, smiling. "That's good."

And then I do snap out of it a little. I start thinking maybe I'm wrong. About the game. About the Raiders. And about the Pats. Maybe I'm wrong about everything except the snow and the rain and the unseasonable cold. Maybe it really is just the weather.

11.

Game 11 vs. Minnesota Vikings

Sunday, November 24, 2002
Record 5–5

So now John figures he understands what I meant about the difference between exciting football and impressive football. I'm glad about that for the most part. I really like it when people have to concede I'm right.

John wasn't so ready to accept my point about impressive and exciting being different when it came up in an e-mail exchange two weeks ago. John, whom I hadn't seen since October 13, the day the Patriots were pasted by the Green Bay Packers, sent me a note asking what I thought about New England's November 10 win over Chicago.

I told him I'd found the victory exciting but unimpressive.

That threw John. "How can a game be exciting without being impressive?" he asked.

"The game was exciting for its very lack of impressiveness," I replied. "Both teams looked awful, only at different times. So it was high scoring and close even though it was mostly a lot of sucky football."

He let it go, but I knew he wasn't convinced.

John is the kind of person who would make a good reporter. Or a scientist. Or a judge. He's smart. He'll listen to what you have to say and consider any point you care to make. But he never quite believes anything unless he's seen the proof of it. And while he'd watched the Patriots-Bears game, he hadn't watched it with my eyes. He hadn't looked at it with an impressive-exciting dichotomy in mind. So he reserved judgment.

John didn't get a chance to test out my theory in the Pats-Raiders game, which was neither exciting nor impressive.

But now he says he gets it. There's a similar split in today's Patriots game against the Minnesota Vikings. It's just shaking out as the opposite of what I saw in the Chicago game.

It's late in the second quarter and the Patriots are sailing toward a certain victory. They've scored three touchdowns, making each of them look easy. Tom Brady hit Christian Fauria for a nine-yard touchdown on the Pats' first drive of the game. He threw another touchdown to Fauria at the start of the second. Then he completed a five-yard touchdown pass to Troy Brown in the middle of the period.

The Pats' defense, meanwhile, has held Minnesota without a score. They've blocked the Vikings' lone field goal attempt. And they've recovered three Minnesota fumbles, the first of which set up Brown's touchdown catch.

It's been impressive as hell, but you wouldn't say the game is exciting. The Vikings always lose on the road. And they commit more turnovers than any team in the league. So what's happening on the field in Foxborough is precisely what was expected.

"This is the difference between impressive and exciting," John says. "The Patriots are winning 21 to nothing—and they should be."

That's the heart of it right there.

For the most part, the lack of excitement in this game is just fine. The Pats are winning big; that's something to be happy about. It's something the team needed desperately after the Oakland game, in which the Patriots failed to score an offensive touchdown. With any luck, the team will keep on rolling right through the afternoon and into its Thanksgiving matchup with Detroit four days from now.

The only problem is that as a result of the game's leisurely feel, it's relatively quiet here at Fritz. Guys are talking, but I don't hear anyone talking about the game. Guys are generally staying attuned to what's happening on TV, but all they have to offer when the Pats do well is mild applause.

It would be hard to muster the energy for any more raucous response to a game this unengaging. But I was hoping for more involvement, more energy—and I'd still like to get it.

I didn't come to Fritz, a gay sports bar in Boston's South End, hoping to shatter stereotypes, but I'd really rather I didn't confirm any. And if things keep up like this, I worry, it's going to be hard to make it clear that this lack of involvement in the game doesn't have anything to do with the anyone's sexual preference.

Andrew, the bartender, may have figured out what I'm thinking. Or maybe he's just worried that a journalist has wandered in on the wrong day. He sets me up with a free beer ("We like to buy every straight guy who comes in here a beer," he says) and tells me he wishes I'd been here for that Bears game. "It was packed," he says, "and it was loud."

There's always a better crowd when the Pats play at four o'clock (as they did against Chicago) than when they're on at one, Andrew assures me.

Some stereotypes are true; the gay bar scene is a late-night scene. And one o'clock on a Sunday afternoon is simply a bit earlier than a lot of Fritz's usual patrons have it in them to get out of bed. Game or no game.

I tell Andrew I'm not worried about it. The crowd is plenty big and getting bigger.

That last part is true. The crowd at Fritz is swelling. It has been since just before kickoff. And I'm sure it's going to keep on growing through the afternoon. But I'm lying about not being worried. Big is one thing. Engaged is quite another. I'd prefer engaged. Hell, I'd prefer to be engaged. I don't have any kind of monetary stake in this game. I need some good football.

Then as the game approaches halftime, the Pats turn the ball over on downs at the Vikings' 29 yard line. And Minnesota's offense comes to life, moving the ball 71 yards in five plays to score a touchdown and bring the game within two scores. I hear some loud cursing from somewhere in the bar as Vikings quarterback Daunte Culpepper throws the touchdown pass to wide receiver D'Wayne Bates. And I think, okay, this is more like it.

I came to Fritz hoping to find an answer to a question that had been bugging me for several weeks. I've spent a lot of time with football fans this season and I've been struck by the level of homophobia

I've encountered. Mostly it's been garden-variety, nondirectional homophobia. That is, no one's been the target of it, it's just been a lot of faceless yahoos yelling "hey faggot" and "you queer" at each other. But while that may be less physically dangerous than outright gay bashing, it's ugly just the same.

I've listened to guys use "fag" and "queer" as insults in and outside of two stadiums, in bars, and on my bus trip to Buffalo. There was the drunken idiot at the End Zone bar in Foxborough opening night who complained that "some queer pinched [his] ass" while he was trying to find a scalper. I watched members of the crowd that same night debate which quarterback is the bigger fag, the Steelers' Kordell Stewart (who has been the subject of persistent rumors about his sexual orientation) or the 49ers' Jeff Garcia, whose speech patterns have a stereotypically gay (read: effeminate) quality about them (and who, you know, plays for San Francisco). I took a 900-mile round trip on a bus with a bunch of classless jackasses who goaded each other to drink with taunts like "What are you, a fag?"

Of the 10 games leading up to today, games I've spent in the company of a wide variety of fans in a mix of settings, there have only been three during which I didn't hear some disparaging remark about gays. For a guy who wants to believe love of an inherently macho game is not incompatible with a progressive social outlook, that's pretty discouraging.

It's even worse than that, though. Because homophobia also apparently pervades the NFL. As with most men's professional sports, football is so hostile to gay players that they remain closeted through their careers, often beyond them. And when a player, even a retired player, comes out, as former defensive lineman Esera Tuaolo did a few weeks earlier, there's invariably a backlash. The fallout from Tuaolo's well-publicized revelation is ongoing. Newspapers are only today reporting that San Francisco 49ers running back Garrison Hearst has finally apologized for antigay statements he made to the *Fresno Bee* after Tuaolo came out.

"I don't want any faggots on my team," the *Bee* quoted Hearst as saying ,"I know this might not be what people want to hear, but that's a punk. I don't want any faggots in this locker room."

Pressure from the 49ers organization and the league forced Hearst to take it back. And that's something, I suppose. It demonstrates that the league and at least one team understand that such expressions of hate can't be tolerated. Of course, cynic that I am, I can't stop wondering whether the official reaction to Hearst's bigotry would have been the same if he played for a team other than the Niners (who have to know where their bread is buttered). I also can't stop wondering why the NFL hasn't taken steps to change the atmosphere in which attitudes like Hearst's are incubated. They can't do it all; the problem obviously reaches back through the NCAA to high school sports and right on into society at large. But that oughtn't stop Commissioner Paul Tagliabue from taking some kind of steps to change what he can.

I haven't read any reports of Hearst being shunned by his teammates or other players, either, as any professional athlete who made a similar statement about an ethnic group surely would have been. John Rocker, another famous professional athlete/bigot, was suspended from baseball in '99, but that was really more a reaction to his expressions of racism than his homophobic and misogynistic output. That says a lot about the regressive state of pro sports. We've done enough to demonstrate that racism is wrong, that sports can't afford to tolerate it. But you can still hate gays (and if you're a male athlete you can still hate and abuse women) and get away with it. It's all made me wonder how gay football fans stick with the game.

My direct question—the one I ask John, one of my oldest friends, and Frank and Anthony, a pair of guys I met only this afternoon here at Fritz—is this: How do you love a game that hates you?

The answer I get from all three men is a good bit simpler than I had expected. It makes me a good bit sadder than I had expected, too. What it boils down to is that there's no point in getting angry at football for something that goes on all around you all the time.

As a straight, white man, someone who has never been subjected to bigotry on any level, I have a hard time getting my head around that. It's all but impossible for me to conceive of being rejected, targeted even, by someone and not come out hating them.

I'm sure there are gay men who hate football (and all of pro sports) for the way they're treated by some athletes and fans. Just as I know there are women who hate everything about the game because of the misogyny and outright abuse some players and fans engage in.

I remember being lectured a few years ago by a woman who had held on to the belief that spousal abuse skyrockets on Super Bowl Sunday (despite the fact that the study "proving" such a spike existed had been long since discredited). She told me the mere fact that I was a football fan proved I was a woman hater. It couldn't be otherwise, she insisted, since I followed a sport that inspired violence toward women.

She was wrong, of course. Not just about me. And not just about the Super Bowl making men beat their wives or girlfriends. But about the game itself. Football doesn't cause men to hate or abuse women. Nor does it encourage them to do so. And the kind of man who beats his wife or girlfriend doesn't need a sport to make him a lowlife.

But I could still understand that woman's anger toward football. It comes from the same place as my embarrassment at the game. It comes from the fact that the football culture—from high school ball to the NFL, from the attitudes in the stands and the bars to the advertising messages on TV—does little to discourage misogyny and much to encourage it. Coaches berate their players when they don't perform well by calling them "girls" or "ladies." Men sit in the stands and make lewd comments to the cheerleaders (whom the team put there to be ogled). Beer ads objectify women so shamelessly that a friend of mine watches football with a remote in hand, ready to change the channel at the start of every commercial break in order to protect his kids from the ugliness. And worst of all, players abuse their spouses and girlfriends with little or no fear of sanction from the league.

And the thing of it is, it's still far more widely accepted in our society to hate gays than it is to hate women. Homophobia doesn't show up on TV commercials, but it shows up just about everywhere else. It shows up on the field and in the locker room (in the form of a culture that keeps people like Tuaolo closeted). It shows up when someone like Hearst makes a hateful statement to the press. It shows up in the stands, the parking lots, and the bars. It shows up to the extent that what's surprising isn't that there are gay men who hate football, but that there are those who can still enjoy it.

Anthony, a fit, athletic-looking guy of about 30, and Frank, a slightly round fellow of about the same age, say they knew they loved football before they knew they were gay. I know the same is true of John and you don't just throw your personality away when you figure out your sexual preference.

"I grew up with football and baseball," Frank tells me. "I led the straight life. I was never one of those queens. I always liked playing sports."

Like a lot of men his age, Frank doesn't participate in sports the way he did as a kid. But he still loves to watch, and he's not about to give that up because it exposes him to a few extra homophobic morons.

"To hell with that," he says. "There's a good amount of gays who are into football and baseball. I have people I can watch a game with."

I could hardly argue with the man while standing in a gay sports bar.

Frank has a thought about Hearst: "He's an asshole."

My favorite thing about Frank is that he's a Pats fan from New Jersey. He has friends in Boston—he, Anthony, and Anthony's boyfriend, Jim, are up visiting them for the weekend—but no real connection to New England. Frank, like Anthony, is mostly a Giants fan. But his AFC team is the Patriots.

"How do you get to be a Pats fan in New Jersey?" I ask him.

"Because I hate the Jets," he offers in a tone so matter of fact, so utterly, easily honest, I can't help but like the guy. Hatred of the Jets is the best qualification I can think of for a Pats fan from outside the region.

My favorite thing about Anthony is that he's completely believable when he tells me he doesn't pay much attention when athletes make homophobic remarks to the press. He hears about it, just like anyone else, but he doesn't get worked up about it. And that's not because he's put up some kind of mental shield. It's because he's got the right point of view about athletes. He likes to watch them on the field, but he doesn't give half a damn about what they think about politics, sexuality, religion, or really anything but the sport they get paid to play.

Hence his take on Hearst: "I could care less what he says. I don't care if he dies. It doesn't faze me in any way."

Anthony, who still plays hockey with friends regularly, says sports are important to him. He doesn't believe that most straight people think like Hearst. Nor does he believe most straight people approve of comments like the one Hearst made. And even if they do, he's not going to let other people's ignorance rob him of something that makes him happy.

It's getting pretty loud in the bar now. The crowd has grown considerably while I've been chatting with Frank and Anthony, so much so, in fact, that I've kind of lost John. He's not physically far away from where I'm sitting, but he's involved in a conversation and he's got his back to me. And there's another group of guys wedged between us, most of them trying to get Andrew's attention.

It's midway through the third quarter and while there hasn't been a score yet in the second half, you can feel that Minnesota is back in the game.

The Pats' two possessions of the quarter have produced all of 35 yards. Brady, who completed 15 of 19 passes in the first half, is two of five since the break. He's been stopped short on an attempt to convert fourth and two. And he's been sacked for a 12-yard loss. That's not helping the ground game any. The Pats running backs are okay, but they're not superstars. They need the threat of a passing game to keep defenders from zeroing in on them. And right now there is no such threat.

The defense has fared slightly better, stopping Minnesota's lone drive of the half after allowing just 15 yards. But special teams have damned near let the D's success go for nothing. Troy Brown muffed a punt at the Pats' 12 yard line after signaling a fair catch. He covered the ball back up again, so there was no real harm done. But plays like that do little to inspire confidence.

I'm not impressed with the Pats team on the field this half. And judging by the sounds of the room, neither are most of the other guys in the bar.

"Come on, Brady," a Tom Selleck look-alike just down the bar to my left shouts impatiently when the quarterback misses Kevin Faulk on second and nine.

"Goddamit!" a more frustrated and passionate voice from somewhere over near the front door yells when defensive tackle Chris Hovan comes in and sacks Brady, bringing up fourth and 21 deep inside New England territory.

And now the Vikings have started a drive on the Patriots' side of the field. They're moving steadily toward their second score of the game.

The Vikings have two talented running backs on their roster. And right now, Moe Williams is the one getting the carries. He goes 14 yards on a second and five and I hear guys here and there around the room yelling, "Stop him, stop him, stop him!" He picks up four yards on the next play, taking the ball to the Patriots' five yard line, and Tom Selleck lets out a frustrated "Come on, Patriots" (he likes that angry "come on" construction). There is applause as Culpepper is sacked for a two-yard loss by defensive end Jarvis Green. But on the next play, the Minnesota quarterback hits wide receiver Kelly Campbell for a touchdown. Loud groans come up from everywhere in the room. Somewhere way off to my left there's a pained "Arrrgh!"

Frank, who has money on the Pats giving eight and a half points, takes a few steps toward the TV nearest us. He could see the set clearly from our spot at the bar, so I can only assume he's hoping his very proximity will somehow throw off the Vikings' attempt at the extra point. It doesn't.

It seems a wasted effort to me. Gary Anderson gets the Vikes to within seven, but even a miss wouldn't have served Frank's purposes. He's going to need the Pats' offense to come back to life if he's going to have a chance to win some money today.

The teams swap field goals to begin the fourth quarter.

The Vikings strike first, with a 38-yarder by Anderson just 14 seconds into the period.

But the Pats' offense kicks in on their next possession. Brady completes passes of 26 and 27 yards to Antowain Smith and full back Marc Edwards, respectively. And while the drive stalls at the Minnesota 16 yard line, Vinatieri's 34-yard kick is good. The bar erupts in a lilting "Let's goooo!" as the ball shoots through the uprights, getting the Pats' lead back up to a touchdown (24–17).

It isn't long thereafter that the crowd is taunting Anderson for missing on a 41-yard attempt with 7:37 left to play. "Yeah!" someone somewhere in the now-packed bar yells out as the ball goes off to the left. "Go Minnesota!" It's not an original or clever comment, but it strikes the right tone and draws laughter from throughout the room.

The Pats get next to nothing out of their next two offensive possessions. Brady hits one of three passes and puts the ball on the ground at the Patriots' 48 yard line. Luckily, Smith is there to recover the fumble and the Patriots end up getting to punt the ball away rather than handing it to the Vikings with great field position.

But Minnesota's lost its offensive fire, too. The Vikings never cross midfield on their last two possessions of the game. And after Culpepper misses tight end Jim Kleinsasser on a desperation attempt to convert fourth and 10 with 17 seconds left in the game, the Pats come out, Brady takes a knee, and the game is over.

Tom Selleck lets out an "Oh, yeah! Yeah!" as Culpepper fails to connect on his fourth-down pass. And Anthony claps his hands once loudly when the last second ticks off the clock. There's some low-key cheering at the end of the game, too. But no one's all that moved. No one can possibly be impressed.

The Pats have won, but they've managed, once again, to look fairly unspectacular in victory.

Unfortunately for Frank, the Pats haven't covered. He can live with that, though. He won his other bet of the day (on the hated Jets) so he's come up pretty close to even.

"It's okay," Frank says. "We needed the win."

"And five more after this," I answer, watching details of the Jets' and Dolphins' victories scroll across the TV screen. Frank offers only a short nod of agreement.

John's found his way back to where I'm sitting and I turn to him. I've got a final thought on the game that only he'll understand.

"So in the end, it was half exciting, half impressive," I say.

John's had his share of gin and tonics and it takes a second for the words to register. But then his eyes light up. "You know," he says, "you're right."

This time just being right isn't quite enough to make me glad. It's good that we got a bit of excitement in the second half, but I'm not at all pleased with the way we got it. On the whole, I'd much rather have been able to say the entire game had proven unexciting but impressive.

Still, the 3–8 Detroit Lions are only four days away. Maybe I'll get an impressive and exciting Patriots win to go along with my turkey dinner. I'd consider that breaking even.

12.

Game 12 at Detroit Lions

Thursday, November 28, 2002
Record 6–5

This has to be the saddest form of Thanksgiving-afternoon entertainment in America. Or maybe it's the second saddest.

The big fun, apparently, is to stick your head in the living room
and get a look at me nodding off in front of the Patriots–Detroit
Lions game. And to see me start and hear me grumble every time I
catch my eyes closing.

I'm in a bad mood. And the fact that I'm dozing just when I
most want to be awake is the better part of the reason for it.

The situation is poetically unjust. After years and years in
which I've had to battle to watch some football on Thanksgiving—while my family has heartlessly insisted I engage in such
lesser pursuits as feasting, chatting, and, you know, all the holiday
togetherness stuff—I'm finally in a setting in which I should be
able to watch all of at least one and maybe both of the NFL's holiday games. My brother, Chris, and his wife, Julie, are hosting
Thanksgiving for the first time. And there's only so much room at
their table. So Chris and I graciously volunteered to eat dinner in
the living room—in front of the TV. We figured it would be a
downhill run from there. When dinner ended, we'd just stay
parked, and the next thing you know it'd be 4:30, time for the
Dallas Cowboys–Washington Redskins game. Only, now it looks
like I'm not going to make it anywhere near the late game.

It's vexing.

I mean, I get how the whole thing is funny. I've got a pretty
good idea of what I must look like, sitting here overstuffed in
the overstuffed, red chair, bloated belly straining against my shirt,
ten-pound bags of exhaustion dragging my eyelids downward,

chin dropping to my chest then snapping back up as I fight to hold on to consciousness. Plus, I understand that football doesn't mean to most of my family what it means to me, and so the fact that I've finally got what I've always wanted only to end up blowing it is nothing but a gas to them.

If something like this were happening to someone else, I'd be the one laughing loudest. Nonetheless, I can't say as I'm particularly amused at the moment.

Of course, I'm also not nearly as far gone as everyone seems to believe. I'm struggling, yes. And I may be destined to lose the fight. But I haven't surrendered just yet. I've managed to keep myself in that transitional state between sleep and wakefulness. I'm not much of a conversationalist like this, but I'm aware of what's happening on the field in Detroit just as I'm aware of the activity in the room around me.

It's not my fault, I want to tell everyone. It's the three glasses of Chateauneuf-du-Pape and the massive overdose of tryptophan. It's having stayed up into the wee hours on each of the three previous nights—one watching Monday Night Football, and then two making pizzelles. And it's the game, too. Because the truth of the matter is, the punt, kick, and turnover competition that's been polluting the TV screen since 12:30 isn't the kind of thing that's likely to keep anyone, anywhere awake. Now that the novelty of looking at the teams' retro uniforms (it's officially Throwback Weekend in the NFL) has worn off, there's no reason to care about a game that's even lamer than the whole "Sean's sleeping" show.

By this time in this season, I've grown relatively accustomed to the Patriots and their sleepy style of football. I've come to expect scoreless quarters, start-stop drives that go on too long and produce no points, even whole games in which the offense never finds the end zone. It's made me wonder at times if the key to some Pats' wins—like the one against Minnesota last Sunday, where they managed to hold on for a victory in the second half without really doing anything particularly well—has been that they've lulled their opponents into some kind of trance. And still, this Thanksgiving game has to be one of the single most boring professional sporting events to which I have ever been witness.

The Lions came into the game looking awful (as has been the team's wont for most of the years that I've been following the NFL). The Patriots came in looking solidly mediocre (also a historical tendency). And neither team has done a thing today to change its image.

It's five minutes into the fourth quarter and nothing has happened since forever. The Pats are ahead 20–9. They've led Detroit since the start of the game. Their opening drive ended in a 31-yard Adam Vinatieri field goal. Two plays later, with 10 minutes remaining on the first-quarter game clock, Tedy Bruschi intercepted Lions quarterback Joey Harrington and went 27 yards into the end zone. That was the last remotely exciting play of the game.

The Patriots' offense has accounted for a total of 275 yards on nine possessions. They've managed a single touchdown, on a drive that started at Detroit's 19 yard line following Harrington's third interception of the first half.

Sure, the defense is having a good day. They've held Detroit to three field goals and forced punts on three other Lions' possessions, two of them from deep in Detroit territory. And they've been on the receiving end of nearly as many Harrington passes as Detroit's wideouts. But stopping Detroit's offense is about as difficult as opening a can of cranberry sauce. And picking off Harrington requires about as much athleticism as mashing potatoes.

Now, Detroit is moving the ball, destined, I imagine, to go nowhere or close to nowhere yet again. I'm sure I wouldn't be leaping to my feet in celebration any time soon even if my belly weren't overfull and my eyes weren't determined to take some time off. But my annoyance at the snickering still has nearly as much to do with the fact that it's a distraction from the game as it does with me being the butt of a joke.

I open my eyes to glare at my sister and then my mother as they hurry out of the room, laughing. I hear someone, maybe it's my sister-in-law, out in the kitchen asking what the joke is. And I hear Chris explain it even as I feel another set of eyes peek in at me. "My brother's struggling to keep his eyes open over there."

I think, "Where the hell are you? You're supposed to be watching the game with me." But I don't have the energy to actually shout it at Chris.

* * *

It's an unfair thought anyhow. To begin with, my brother never actually promised to watch the game with me. I assumed he'd try since he's always in the past been the next person after me to creep away from the dinner table to sneak in a few minutes of game time. But I knew it would be tough for him to pull off this year.

Hosting Thanksgiving dinner is a pretty big job, even for the smallish group (10 in all) gathered here at Chris and Julie's Uxbridge home. And while the turkey's been cooked, carved, and served, there's still coffee to brew, pies and cakes to cut, and cookies to put out. There's also the cleanup from dinner.

If the game had turned out to be a nail-biter, an air show, even an honest-to-God Patriots rout, the dishes might have been left to sit for another hour. But I can hardly blame my brother for wanting to get a head start on the pile when there's only this mess to miss.

He's put in his time, anyhow. Dinner didn't start until after 2 P.M. There was a good hour and a half of football before that, and my brother spent it moving between the living room and the kitchen. A few plays, then a look at the squash. A few more and a check on the turkey. Chris missed one of Detroit's field goals while he was greeting our parents. We both missed Tom Brady throwing an interception while we were carrying pies in from our Aunt Deb's car.

As dinnertime approached and the game dragged onward, even I found other things more interesting than football. Late in the second half, with the turkey out of the oven and sitting while its juices set, my mother conducted a clinic on how to make gravy. Flour to thicken the drippings, then broth to thin the mix. A wire whisk in slow constant motion to prevent lumps.

"My problem is that I always make it way too thick," I told Mom. "I always think I need a lot more flour than I do. Like, I keep adding it because the gravy never seems to get thicker, then all at once it's like mud."

In classic motherly fashion, she told me what she knew I already knew: "You just have to be patient." I've heard that before. It's never taken yet.

Glancing over my shoulder at the TV just in time to see the Patriots set up to punt on fourth and seven from their own 48, I thought, "The Pats care less about winning than we do about when to add flour." It probably wasn't true. They probably wanted to win every bit as much as any of us ever wanted to make a perfect turkey gravy.

Once my Mom finished her gravy and Chris finished carving his gorgeous bird, we piled our plates as high as reasonably possible with turkey, potatoes, stuffing, squash, and cranberry sauce and hightailed it to the living room. Even then, with halftime fast approaching, neither of us was exactly enthralled with the action on the field. But we'd been handed an opportunity and we were damned well going to take it.

We shared cooking secrets and talked about the approaching holidays while Bon Jovi yowled from the TV at halftime. We worked on second helpings of dark meat, potatoes, and stuffing as the Pats and Lions stumbled through the beginning of the third quarter, each team doing its best not to play any actual football.

Midway through the period, with the Pats leading 17–6, my mother popped in. "Who's winning?"

"New England," Chris and I muttered together.

"Oh," Mom answered, looking a bit surprised. "I don't hear a lot of screams."

"Not a lot to scream about," I mumbled, barely looking up from my plate.

On the TV, the officials announced that a Patriots challenge of a 16-yard completion by Harrington had been successful; the ball was called back. But on the next play, Harrington completed a nine-yard pass for an indisputable first down. And the Lions, though no one could accuse them of having a good day, continued to move the ball a chunk at a time, edging toward their third field goal.

As the kick went up, bringing Detroit within eight points, neither Chris nor I had any reason to be confident that the Patriots would hold on for the win. We had a good idea Detroit would hold on for the loss, but that isn't quite the same.

Chris decided the retro Patriots uniforms were bringing bad luck. Though earlier in the day he'd been excited to see the team's original mascot, Pat Patriot—"Look, it's the Sam Cunningham," he exclaimed as the Pats trotted onto the field in uniforms that reminded him of the running back from our youth—it had subsequently occurred to him that the Patriots who wore those colors weren't anything like the Patriots who won Super Bowl XXXVI. They were more like the floundering, ineffective bunch we were watching this Thanksgiving at Ford Field.

When Adam Vinatieri put up his second field goal of the day at the beginning of the fourth quarter, giving the Pats a 20–9 lead and a solid grip on an awful game, Chris made for the kitchen. I settled in, leaned back, and started to feel the weight of my eyelids.

I'd always heard about people needing naps after a big Thanksgiving dinner, but I don't think I'd ever felt the pull of slumber. I suppose I was always too excited about getting away from the table in time for the late game.

Football has been a part of Thanksgiving since before football was football. It's been a part of the holiday for almost as long as there's been an official, government-sanctioned Thanksgiving.

Thanksgiving was established as an annual celebration in 1863, when Abraham Lincoln decreed that it should be observed on the fourth Thursday of November. The first Thanksgiving football game was played 13 years later, when the newly formed Intercollegiate Football Association held its first championship game on the holiday. (Yale beat Columbia, two touchdowns to none.) But the game played that day was more like a blend of European football (soccer) and rugby than the modern game. And while American football went through a dramatic evolutionary period in the 1880s—the period during which Yale medical student and half back Walter Camp developed much of the structure that endures today—Thanksgiving continued to be a day when important college games were played.

The game Camp developed quickly spread outside the Ivy League schools where it was first played. And so did the tradition of the Thanksgiving game. By the turn of the 19th century, there were more than 5,000 collegiate, scholastic, and club football games being played every fourth Thursday in November.

The first professional football game played on Thanksgiving took place in 1920. The Akron Pros topped the Canton Bulldogs 7–0. Fourteen years later, the Chicago Bears beat the Lions 19–16 in the NFL's first-ever Thanksgiving game. That game also marked the beginning of the league's vital connection to electronic media, as NBC radio became the first network to offer a nationwide broadcast of an NFL game.

Detroit has hosted an NFL game nearly every Thanksgiving since the day they lost to the Bears. Dallas began its run as the other NFL holiday host city in 1966.

For me, Thanksgiving has always been linked to football in one form or another. When I was a kid, we'd almost always start the holiday with Milford High School's match against its traditional Thanksgiving Day rival, Shrewsbury. Those games were morning games, so they didn't interfere with dinner. And I'm fairly certain Dad's job was to take us somewhere so we'd be out of the way as Mom prepared whatever she'd been charged with bringing to my grandmother's house.

I never saw NFL Thanksgiving games in those days, because they were never on at Gram's. When I was very young, I'd play with my brother and sister after dinner as the adults chatted and played Michigan rummy for pennies. As we kids got older, we got to be part of the card game. The TV would often be on in the living room, but it was always tuned to some movie; there may as well have been no game.

Michigan rummy disappeared from our family holiday tradition sometime in the early '80s. Everyone just sort of grew bored with it, I guess. By then I was a teenager, too, and I was becoming more and more rabid about pro football. I started finding ways to get away from the dinner table and catch parts of the two games.

A few years after I was graduated from high school, when it stopped being fun to go to the Milford games just to run into friends home from college for the holiday, the pro games became the only football I could get on Thanksgiving. Chris and I started barricading ourselves in Aunt Deb's TV room as soon as we could escape from the table. We usually got to see the last part of the early game and as much of the late game as we could manage. Of course, there were always interruptions, always demands.

"Come on and have dessert at the table," Mom would implore. "It's a holiday. Can't you turn the TV off for half an hour and come spend time with your family?"

We could. But we didn't want to.

As adulthood set in, I grew more and more to understand the importance of spending time with family when you can. But I never grew out of the desire to catch as much football as possible on Thanksgiving. I've maintained for years that there's no reason we shouldn't have the TV on in the dining room. With the sound down, of course. I know I'm horribly wrong about it, but I want it just the same.

Or at the very least, I've always thought I wanted it. But I've thought that with images in my mind of Barry Sanders scoring three touchdowns in the Lions' '97 win over the Bears, of Randy Moss getting three scores a year later to lift the Vikings over the Cowboys, and of Leon Lett single-handedly ruining what should have been a clutch victory for his Cowboys over the Dolphins in '93. I didn't think it considering the Cowboys' painful 20–17 victory over the Patriots in '84. Or the 34–9 shellacking the Lions put on the Pats in their only other holiday meeting, on Thanksgiving Day 2000.

And I sure as hell didn't think it imagining the kind of stale, stupefying display I've inexplicably been striving to stay awake for today.

I'm still in an odd state of semialertness as Detroit lines up for their fourth field goal of the game. We're five minutes into the fourth quarter.

Jason Hanson hits from 46 yards out, bringing the Lions back within eight points. That gap would be surmountable for any real professional football team with nearly 10 minutes of playing time remaining, but it's more than enough to keep the game entirely out of reach for Detroit.

Even so, I come back to full consciousness as the kick goes up. But that's not really because of the game. It's because my brother-in-law, David, and his mother, Ardath, have finished eating and have joined me in the living room.

As far as David and Ardath know, this may well be the most exciting, well-played football game of the season. All they see is a Lions field goal followed by a nine-and-a-half-minute, clock-devouring Patriots drive that starts at New England's 19 yard line and moves all the way to the Lions' one yard line. It's an awkward

drive, studded with penalties on both sides of the ball (an encroach-
ment call here, a delay of game there, until the drive becomes an extended tango of five-yard walk-offs), but it makes the Pats' offense
look almost okay. Brady hits Troy Brown and Daniel Graham on a
couple of nice pass plays. Marc Edwards, Kevin Faulk, and Antowain Smith all contribute short gains on the ground.

It's enough to get Ardath excited. And her enjoyment of the
drive picks me up a bit, not least of all because she's someone I
never would have pegged as a football fan. I don't know Ardath
well, but I know she's an artsy type from the woods of western
Massachusetts. We have a lot of those in my part of the state, and
I've known very few of them to be football fans. It's fun to discover that people are not exactly who you thought they were.

With just less than five minutes left in the game, the Pats start to
stall out at the Lions' 34 yard line. Brady overthrows Graham on
first down. Smith takes a two-yard loss on second. Then, facing
third and 12, Brady hits Troy Brown for a nice 17-yard pickup.

"Yeah!" Ardath half shouts. "They needed that."

Three plays later Brady steps up again, turning a broken play
on third and seven into an eight-yard pickup and a first down.
There are three and a half minutes remaining. I think about calling Chris and my father in from the kitchen to watch the end of
the game, but they're in the middle of a conversation about gut-
ters or something and I decide it isn't worth interrupting.

Ardath, for her part, wants to see the Pats finish strong.

"They'd better get a touchdown after all this," she says.

"Yeah," I grumble. "I'd like to see them finish off one of their
drives."

She stays positive—"I know, it's been a great drive"—but even
that doesn't last.

At the Detroit one yard line with 31 seconds remaining in the
game, the Pats approach the ball clearly not intending to finish the
day off with a score.

"They should try to get a touchdown," Ardath argues.

"They're just gonna let the clock run down," David tells her.

"Oh, come on!" she offers in disbelief.

I know just exactly how she's feeling.

The Pats have done just enough to get by the Detroit Lions, a team whose win-loss average is quickly headed for the bad side of the Mendoza Line.

And I'm not interested in hearing arguments about how Detroit always plays tough on Thanksgiving. Assuming the Patriots don't find a way to lose in the final half-minute today, the Lions will be 30–28–2 on the day. That includes the stretch in the '50s and early '60s when they beat up on the hapless, pre–Vince Lombardi Green Bay Packers every Thanksgiving. That's not tough; that's average. Plus, the Lions who hosted the Patriots today are, pure and simple, one of the worst teams in the league.

The rest of the Pats' schedule won't be so easy. They've got Buffalo in 10 days. That might not be too bad. The Bills haven't won a game since before the Pats thumped them in Buffalo a month ago. But Drew Bledsoe will be anxious to put on a show in his return to Foxborough, and if the Patriots play like they did today, they'll lose. Then things get tougher as New England faces the Tennessee Titans, the Jets, and the Dolphins. As of right now, every one of those teams has a shot at the play-offs. And two of them, the division rival Jets and Fins, will know they've got to beat the Patriots if they're going to make the postseason.

Brady takes a knee and the clock runs down to the buzzer. They've won the game. They've covered the spread. There was no reason to try a sneak or even a field goal at the last second. Except that it might have made the game just a little more fun to watch.

I watch the teams walk off the field. And two minutes later, I'm grabbing a piece of apple pie, aiming to catch at least part of what I hope will be a better game between Washington and Dallas, and filling Chris in on the retro Pats' frustrating retro finish.

"What happened today?" he asks.

"The same damned thing that's been happening for the last two months," I tell him. "The Pats couldn't be bothered to play football."

"That's no good," he says. Then, "I'm telling you, it was those uniforms."

"Probably," I say, because what are you going to do in that situation, argue? Besides, maybe he's right. I mean, I don't remember seeing Pat Patriot anywhere the day I saw the Broncos pound the Pats. Nor do I recall him being on hand for the Raiders game. Or the Bears or Vikings games, either. But maybe he was. Maybe the Pats have somehow connected with the spirit of the teams of the '70s and '80s.

If that's the case, they'd best find their way back to 2002 in a hurry. Because there are four games ahead against teams that have never left it. And if the Pats don't win at least three of them, their 2003 is going to be nine months coming.

13.

Game 13 vs. Buffalo Bills

Sunday, December 8, 2002
Record 7–5

For the most part, I was feeling lucky. Weird, but lucky. Except for the matter of one giant booger. It sat there staring at me, daring me to turn to the left, calling me to check every now and again to see if it was still there. It always was. And after a while it got to be much too late to say anything to the guy whose nose it was hanging out of (if indeed there was ever a good time).

But I'm getting to the booger too soon. Better, I think, to back up and start somewhere near the beginning.

It was an odd day, different in virtually every way from what I'd imagined.

To begin with, I'd woken up feeling good about the Pats. And that had become an unfamiliar feeling.

It had been quite a few weeks since I went into a game day in a positive frame of mind about the home team—at least since the day of the Chicago game, when the team was coming off a big win over Buffalo, and probably since the day of the Kansas City game 11 weeks ago.

Heading into that game against the Chiefs, the Pats looked like they could repeat as league champions. They appeared to have lost neither drive nor momentum. They'd won 11 straight games, going back to November 2001. And it felt like they were ready to continue their streak for at least another month.

But things fell apart. The Pats barely got out of the Kansas City game with a win. And while I still thought they could get back on track with their game in San Diego the next week, I no longer believed anything was certain.

It wasn't. The Pats' defense lost the ability to stop the run. Their offense lost its spark almost entirely. The Patriots went from being one of the NFL's elite squads to being just another football team struggling to end its season with more wins than losses. They started looking like the Patriots I'd always known and felt vaguely, pityingly warm toward.

On this day, though, I had a sense things would be better.

Maybe it was just because the Bills were in town. The Pats had thoroughly dominated Buffalo in their November 3 game at Ralph Wilson Stadium. Logic suggested New England would probably fare at least as well on their own turf. Plus, I hadn't forgotten about Don's theory that Bill Belichick has Drew Bledsoe's number.

Still, the Bills had beaten Miami by a score of 38–21 in their December 1 match. And the Dolphins had bettered the Pats in their last meeting. So there was never any reason to believe that Buffalo couldn't beat New England. I just sort of had the notion that they wouldn't.

It could also have been the fact that the Patriots were back in contention for the AFC East championship. The Dolphins, with their loss to the Bills, had dropped to 7–5, the same record as the Pats. And since my Raiders had defeated the hated Jets, that meant the Pats and Fins were tied for the best record in the division. So as long as the Pats could keep winning, they'd have the chance to take the East in their season-ending game against Miami at Gillette Stadium.

None of that made me any more impressed with what the Pats had done on the field in most of their last 10 games, but I couldn't argue with the numbers. Tied for first is tied for first. And even I, the most stubborn of pessimists, could only take a measure of hope from that.

Or it might have been nothing more than an odd side effect of the onset of holiday cheer and the blessing of unseasonably warm weather. After weeks of early winter, of bitter cold, of biting winds, and of far, far too much snow, the climate in New England had turned distinctly milder. It was still uncomfortably cold when I left home at 10 A.M., shivering as I drove down the street waiting for my car's heater to kick in, but I knew it would be fairly pleasant by game time. The sky was overcast, but not threatening. And with the hint of Christmas in the clean, clear air, it would have been difficult not to experience a certain amount of joie de vivre.

Whatever it was that brought it on, my positive sense about the day ahead was as pleasant as it was unexpected.

It was also odd that I ended up in Gillette Stadium.

I'd spent the week trying to arrange to get together with a group of women Pats fans. One of them, a woman my sister knows from work, said she thought they might be open to letting a man sit in for a game. And at least at first, they were. But then they canceled at the last minute, telling me they just weren't going to get together for the Bills game. I wasn't sure I bought the excuse, but I could only accept it.

So I drove out to Foxborough, figuring I'd walk the parking lots and see what I could see. I thought I might run into some tailgaters somewhere who didn't have tickets and who were planning to stay outside and watch the game in their RV. I figured maybe I could talk them into taking me in. Or maybe I could bribe them into it. I picked up a case of Guinness bottles and a couple of fresh, locally made kielbasas on my way out of town, thinking they might make me a more desirable guest.

I parked behind the End Zone bar and worked my way up Route 1, approaching fans at every RV I passed. Most were friendly. Some were weirded out. In the parking lot where I'd spent the morning of the Kansas City game with the guys in the bus, I talked to a big, bearded guy who clearly didn't need any of the beer in my trunk. He couldn't get his head around what I was asking.

"I don't have an extra ticket," he told me, standing just outside his RV.

"I'm not looking for a ticket," I tried to explain. "I'm trying to find people who stay in their RV during the game."

"No, I can't do that," he said, then, motioning back toward the door. "I've got to go with these guys."

"Oh, okay, so you're all going to the game?"

"Yeah, that's why we're here. For the game."

"But you're all going in. No one's staying out here."

"How much do you want to give me?"

"For what?"

"For my ticket. How much?"

"I don't want your ticket. I want to find somebody who isn't going in to the game."

"So you can buy their ticket."

"No, so I can watch the game with them."

"How are you gonna watch the game if you don't have a ticket?"

It was time to move on. "Hey, uh, enjoy the game, okay? I've gotta go."

As I walked away I started to feel bad. I'd confused some poor drunk dude with a weird request, then got impatient with him for failing to understand me. So I turned to say "Go Pats" or something like that. But he was already climbing back into his RV.

I imagined the exchange he must have been having with his friends inside: "Who was that?" "I don't know. Some guy who wanted to buy my ticket."

I got to thinking I'd made a mistake going to Foxborough. I should have just parked myself at a nice cozy sports bar somewhere. And I decided that my best bet was to head for the End Zone and see if I couldn't hook up with some of the gang from the Monday night opener.

But on my way back to my car, I fell ass backward into a ticket.

The Children's Hospital in Boston had volunteers out in the parking lots and along Route 1 collecting donations. And I'd dropped a five into a canister shortly after pulling in to town, so I wasn't really looking at the table set up at the entrance to one of the lots. In fact, I was doing my best not to look at it. If I'd made eye contact with one of the workers, I'd have felt like I needed to take out my wallet or explain that I'd already given. And in a situation like that, I figure they assume "I gave down the road" is a lie. Most of the time it probably is.

But you can't avert your ears. So I couldn't miss the fact that one of the volunteers had a ticket for sale. Someone—not, I assumed, the bearded guy from the RV—had donated a ticket. And the hospital fund-raisers were looking to sell it.

The guy calling out that he had a ticket for sale saw me looking at him.

"Sir, do you need a ticket?" he asked.

"The money goes to the hospital?" I said.

"That's right."

"How much are you hoping to get for it?"

"Just face value," he said. "Seventy-five dollars."

"You sure?" I asked. "You could probably get more."

"I'm not a scalper," he laughed. Then he explained. "We got it for nothing. Seventy-five dollars is a good donation."

"It's a good seat," he added. If he'd been a salesman, someone would have had to teach him to stop selling once you've closed the deal.

I gave him $100, figuring my good luck and his good cause had to be worth a 33 percent markup. I brushed off the thank-yous (feeling like it's not really charity if you get something in return) and headed for Gillette.

I wondered as I hurried up Route 1, pushing my way into the increasingly dense pedestrian traffic, whether the seat I'd bought really was as good as the Children's Hospital guy had promised. I didn't care about seating charts when I was buying the ticket, but now I couldn't help but think about where section 240 might be.

I got distracted for a bit as I stood in a thick crowd of people waiting to cross the highway. It was just more interesting to eavesdrop on conversations about Bledsoe; the Tennessee Titans, the dangerous, streaking AFC South team that's next on the Patriots' schedule; and Miami Dolphins quarterback Jay Fiedler. I learned that "Bledsoe sucks," the Titans are overrated, and Fiedler is either a "fag" or a "pussy" (the guy doing the talking apparently was having a hard time choosing between homophobia and misogyny—admittedly, a tough call).

For a few seconds, I contemplated giving even more money to the Children's Hospital. A quiet little girl, maybe nine years old, who was working the crowd as it waited to cross Route 1, was having a tough time getting people's attention. Plus, she was working a tough spot, the end of a long line of fund-raising stations along the pedestrian route to the stadium. Then I watched in amusement as a state trooper called her over to where a guy who might have been 40 or so stood with an open wallet and a sheepish look on his face. He'd been caught with an open container of alcohol in a public place (a violation of Massachusetts law) and given the opportunity to atone with an act of charity.

"Keep in mind, sir, that's a $40 fine—when you make your donation," the statey prodded. I joined a crowd of people chuckling over the scene as other troopers stopped traffic and waved us across the street.

Heading down the walkway to the stadium, I ran into a couple of actual scalpers. I wanted to ask what they were getting for their tickets, just for future reference, but I didn't want to push my luck. What if the second I stopped to ask the question, one of those state troopers came along and assumed I was actually looking to buy? I don't know what the fine is for buying a scalped ticket, but I assumed it was probably pretty steep. And charity does have its limits.

My seat turned out to be near the top of the uppermost section in the end zone nearest Route 1. It wasn't the best seat in the house, but I've sat in worse. And, you know, I was in the stadium. I wasn't in a living room somewhere feeling like an intruder and making a bunch of women I didn't know uncomfortable. I wasn't at the End Zone trying to explain to Louis how I was a believer for the day. And I wasn't sitting in an RV trying to explain to a bewildered drunk that I still didn't want his ticket.

I was on hand for a game that was destined to sell out the minute Bledsoe has been traded to Buffalo. And I was in for about a third of what I would have had to pay a scalper.

Plus, the day had turned out to be warmer than it had any business being, somewhere in the mid-40s. On December 8 in New England, that's about as good as it gets. The overcast had cleared a bit, too, and the sunlight on my face felt good. It wasn't like I was going to start shedding layers of clothing, but I did put my gloves in my pocket. And I unbuttoned my coat.

The crowd around me up in the back rows of section 240 was both entertaining and energetic.

A group of young cops from Worcester, seated just behind me in row 27, were a lot of fun to listen to, partially because they were forever locked in friendly arguments with each other, and partially because they were a little bit mean.

They argued over whether Notre Dame's football team deserved its 11th-place poll ranking, engaging in the kind of unsubstantiated debate you hear in bars, the kind where it's obvious that all that's going on is that one guy loves a team and the other hates it.

"They're definitely better than Washington State," one of them insisted.

"No, they're not," his buddy shot back.

"They're better than Oklahoma," the first tried.

"No, they're not. You think they're ranked too low? They're too high. They shouldn't be ahead of Michigan."

"They beat Michigan."

"Yeah, barely. And they lost to BC and USC."

"That doesn't matter. They've got a better record than Michigan, they beat Michigan. How can you say they're not as good as Michigan?"

"Because they suck."

"We'll just have to agree to disagree."

"That's because you don't know what you're talking about."

They argued about whether the attention-loving woman in row 19 was good looking. (Her suggestive dancing and other antics, they'd tell me later, are a regular thing. They're season-ticket holders and so is she—they call her Dirty Girl.)

They discussed their various bets on the game. They poked fun relentlessly at passers-by, players on the field, and one another.

When cornerback Otis Smith, who's been having a tough season, tackled Bills wide receiver Peerless Price at the Bills' 40 yard line (after a pickup of nine yards), one of them mockingly shouted, "Otis!"

"He fell on him by accident," the guy next to him added.

When a guy in his early 20s with spiked hair and lots of piercings came walking up the stairs, one of them wondered, "Is this the club or the game?"

"How much hair spray do you think he used?" another asked.

"To come to a Pats game," a third chimed in.

* * *

The rest of the section was in a celebratory mood. They danced to the bad music that pumped out of the stadium's sound system during time-outs. They high-fived and hugged each other when the Pats played well (which happened a lot). Dirty Girl threw miniature candy canes into the crowd.

Then there was Len, a major Pats fan who had the seat immediately to my left.

Len was covered in Pats gear: a cap that lit up, a jacket with his name embroidered on the breast, a pair of blue-and-red warm-up pants, and a Ty Law game jersey that he unzipped his jacket to show off when Law made a big play. He was friendly. He was positive. He was charged up. And he had a great big chunk of semicongealed yellow snot hanging from a tuft of hair at the tip of his right nostril. That was a problem.

I noticed the booger almost as soon as I sat down. I'd made it into the stadium just slightly later than I would have liked. I missed the coin toss while I was searching for section 240. When I found my seat, I turned to ask Len which team had won the toss (it was the Pats) and I saw it hanging there.

For a while, I just sort of sat there, eyes focused on the field, doing everything in my power not to glance over at it. Not knowing what to do. You can't just tell some guy you don't know that he's got a booger hanging out of his nose. Well, maybe some people can. But I can't. All I could do was try not to look at it and hope Len would notice it on his own. Or that he'd just blow his nose or something.

Only, Len didn't notice, and he didn't blow his nose. So it just continued to be there. And I started to think maybe I should say something after all. The guy would be embarrassed, probably, but I'd really be doing him a favor. Plus, maybe I was already making him uncomfortable by sitting there refusing to look at him when he made comments about the game. There was also this: What if something really exciting had happened on the field and he snorted or something? I could have ended up wearing the thing.

I kept thinking of the filthy, smelly guy my friend Tom ended up sitting next to the day the Pats lost to Denver, and the drunk who threw up on my buddy Ken years ago at a play-off game between the Raiders and Bills in Buffalo. I kept thinking maybe it was my turn.

The Pats were having a good day. In the first half, the offense scored four times (two well-executed passing touchdowns and two field goals), and the D picked off two of Bledsoe's passes. That led to a lot of high-fiving with Len and the cops in row 27. And a lot of seeing the booger.

At halftime, Len left to get a beer. And as soon as he was out of earshot, the guys in 27 started talking about the booger. I turned and told them it was scaring me. Assuming Len and I had come to the game together, they asked me why I hadn't said something to my buddy.

"I don't know the guy," I told them. "What the hell do you say? Hey, buddy, nice to meet you. Do you know you've got a great big piece of snot hanging out of your nose?"

One of the cops, a guy named Gary, who had been one of the loudest of the bunch, resolved to take one for the team and say something to Len on his return. But he chickened out. Len came back with a fresh beer and an aging booger. And as the third quarter progressed, I could only be thankful that the Bills were creeping back into the game. (Mike Hollis hit a 26-yard field goal and Bledsoe threw a 12-yard touchdown pass.) It made for less celebrating, which allowed me to keep my eyes focused forward.

Meanwhile, the guys in 27 got really nasty. "My daughter is terrified of the boogeyman," Gary announced loudly at one point. "She thinks the boogeyman is under her bed."

The other three snickered. And then they all snickered some more.

And every time Buffalo did something well, the lot of them would break into a chorus of, "That's snot fair."

It was ugly, childish, churlish behavior. And it was unavoidably funny. I laughed at their inane, mean-spirited jokes even as I felt horrible for doing it. And I realized there was no longer any possibility that anyone would tell Len about his situation. I thought about how he'd feel later on when he looked in a mirror and saw the snot. I wondered if he'd remember all the weird comments he'd heard during the game, whether he'd realize there was a reason I could never look at him for very long. I wondered if he'd be hurt or angry. And I wondered how many times in my life people had made fun of me for something. I decided I was learning what it must be like to be a high school bully. I felt small, mean, and bad about myself. And still, I kept on not telling Len to blow his nose.

In the fourth quarter, the Pats retook control of the game. Otis Smith forced and then recovered a fumble a minute and a half into the period (without a smart-ass comment from the guys in row 27, who were too busy making fun of some guy in a camouflage jacket). Antowain Smith ran four yards for a touchdown a few minutes of game time later. And then the D intercepted Bledsoe two more times.

At the two-minute warning, with the Pats leading 27–10, the cops got up to leave. I waited a few seconds then moved back a row. I smiled at a guy who walked by and asked, "How do you like first place?" I watched Buffalo score a meaningless touchdown with 1:09 left in the game. After that, the Bills tried an on-side kick, but the Pats recovered. Len got up to leave and I missed my last chance to give him a heads up about the booger. I watched Tom Brady take a knee twice, killing the clock and ending the game. Then I headed for the parking lot, feeling like an asshole.

I was still feeling mostly lucky. It had been a good day. I'd enjoyed a pleasant December afternoon watching a game I should never have got into. I gave some money to a worthy cause. And I found a reason to have hope for the Patriots.

Sure, the Pats had looked like champions the last time they played Buffalo, only to go right back to being an average team in the weeks that followed. But maybe December would make the difference. Maybe with the division championship and a chance to get back to the Super Bowl in sight, they'd find the magic that made the last part of their 2001 season so exciting.

The NFL is a different league in December than it is in September, October, and November. Teams that have walked through their first 12 games break into sprints over their final four. They hit the play-offs running and they never stop. The Pats team that manhandled Buffalo could easily be that kind of team. The up-coming Monday night game at Tennessee suddenly looked entirely winnable.

All of that should have had me feeling grand.

But as I walked back to my car, as I sat in traffic on Route 1, and as I made the long drive back home to Northampton, all I could think about was how I hadn't done the decent, if difficult, thing before the Bills ever completed their opening kickoff.

After all, I thought, we're supposed to be some kind of com-munity, right? Fans cheering together, celebrating together, maybe looking out for one another. For the first time in weeks, the Patri-ots hadn't disappointed their fans. So some of us just went ahead and disappointed ourselves.

14.

Game 14 at Tennessee Titans

Monday, December 16, 2002
Record 8–5

Kerrie made a bold prediction. And although she didn't intend for me to hear it, she was glad, at least initially, to know that I had.

"They're gonna score a touchdown," Kerrie said as the Patriots lined up on third down at the Tennessee Titans' 10 yard line.

If she'd left it at that, I would have chalked it up to plain old fan talk. But Kerrie didn't leave it at that. She took it one giant leap further.

"If they get a touchdown right now, they're gonna win the game."

That's what really drew my attention. Sure, it was fan talk just like the first prediction, but on a much grander scale. And unlike the run-of-the-mill stuff I've become accustomed to hearing in bars. It was irresistibly intriguing. Alluringly curious. It made me wonder if maybe Kerrie and I were watching different Patriots teams play different Titans teams in different Monday Night Football games. There were more TVs than I could count, never mind watch, arranged around the bar at the Sports Depot. Maybe Kerrie had fixed on a set that was showing a game from some weird parallel dimension—one where the Pats were actually making an effort to win.

In the game I was watching, there was absolutely no reason to believe the Patriots had any chance of reaching the end zone. They could get a first down at the Tennessee six yard line; that seemed remotely possible. And it was a pretty safe bet Adam Vinatieri, one of the league's best placekickers, would hit the 27-yard field goal even if they didn't gain a yard. So some points were likely.

But it was a little more than halfway through the game and the Pats had yet to find the end zone. Moreover, the New England offense had barely moved the ball in the first two quarters, gaining a mere 78 yards in four possessions. That's why it struck me as a bit overly optimistic to think they would put up six points from 10 yards out two minutes into the third quarter.

That's how things looked in my reality anyhow. But, as I said, there was always the possibility that Kerrie had found a signal from a somewhat happier plane.

Kerrie hadn't been talking to me, anyway (she didn't really seem to be talking to anyone). So I didn't argue the point. I just kept watching the game. And the next thing I saw was Tom Brady running up the middle, passing the first-down marker and zipping forward into the end zone.

Touchdown.

The massive crowd gathered around the Sports Depot's enormous bar roared. I took a few seconds to absorb the scene. Then I turned to Kerrie.

"You called it," I said. "That was amazing."

She turned her head to look at me, every inch of her face engaged in a giant smile.

"I did!" Kerrie said with a hearty nod. "You heard that?"

"Oh, yeah, I heard it."

Her head spun back to her left. "I called it," she told her friend Jaime. Then, gesturing toward me with a short head bob, "He heard me."

She turned back to face me. "I did it once before," she said. "I said if they score a touchdown on this play, they'll win the game. And they did."

"So you think they're gonna win now?"

Kerrie looked at me as if I were crazy for asking, as if it didn't matter that the Pats were still down 14–7 in a road game in which they weren't playing well by any standard. She had just one word for me: "Yup." And she punctuated her point with a swig of her Bud Light.

A minute later, with the commercial break over and the Pats preparing for the kickoff, Kerrie turned to me again.

"I'm glad you heard me," she said. Then, to clarify, "I'm glad someone heard me. No one ever listens to me."

I didn't need to see Kerrie's big grin to know the statement wasn't meant as some sort of sad sack's lament. I would have recognized the sentiment anywhere, having felt it myself a thousand times.

It was a football-fan thing. Deep down, all serious football fans believe we know the game better than just about anyone. We believe we can predict the outcome of any given play, or any given game, better than anyone around us. Deeper still, we all know we're full of shit. But that doesn't stop us from feeling like unrecognized geniuses, especially on those occasions when we successfully predict what's going to happen on the field. It doesn't matter how many other predictions we've made that have been wrong; we want recognition for that odd good call. And we're convinced no one's ever going to give it to us.

It was satisfying, then, to be able to offer some momentary validation to a fellow fan. Even if she was a perfect stranger who just happened to be sitting next to me at a bar. Even if it was abundantly clear that Kerrie's broader prediction, that the Pats were on their way to victory, could only be completely off the mark. Or at least that was the case in my reality.

Kerrie was hardly the only person at the Sports Depot who believed the Pats had begun a comeback with their first drive of the second half. In fact, as far as I know, I was the sole person in the crowded bar who believed otherwise. Never mind that the Pats' 69-yard march down the field to the touchdown was aided by two 15-yard penalties against the Titans. Never mind that Brady, who completed seven of 13 passes in the first half, still wasn't throwing the ball very well. All that mattered to the fans around me was the fact that the Patriots had cut the Titans' lead in half. So I was alone in a very big crowd.

The Sports Depot, which bills itself as "Boston's Best Sports Bar," isn't what you'd call cozy. The gorgeous dark-wood bar itself is bigger than a lot of barrooms, and even that doesn't fill as much as half of the converted train station. There's a large dining area you have to pass through on your way to the bar. And beyond the bar area there is what looks to be some kind of function room. Most of the crowd was gathered around the bar, though, watching the game on the big-screen TV by the edge of the dining area or on one of dozens of smaller (read: normal-sized) sets suspended from metal rigging above the bar or stationed on shelves that line the Sports Depot's walls. Throughout much of the game, the crowd stood three and four deep all around the bar, ensuring that the guys mixing drinks never had an idle moment in which to take in some of the game. There were easily 300 people in the room.

I really didn't mind the idea that I was the only person in a rather sizable bunch who had come to expect a Titans win. Actually, I kind of liked it. I was still hopeful that I might be wrong about the Pats' chances of turning things around in the second half. And the team clearly needed all the positive energy fans could pour out into the night.

The game in Tennessee was a crucial one for the Pats. Although they'd gone into the weekend tied with Miami for first place in the AFC East, the Dolphins had moved up half a game on Sunday with a win over the Raiders. And the Pats needed to keep pace with Miami.

If they could beat the Titans and then, in a week, the Jets, the Patriots would go into their last game of the season, at home against Miami, with the ability to win the division simply by winning the game. That is, as the late-season cliché goes, they would control their own destiny. But if they fell a game back with a loss to Tennessee, things would get complicated. They'd need a week 16 win over the Jets coupled with a Dolphins loss to the terrible Minnesota Vikings to get matters back under control. Otherwise, at best, they'd end up playing their final game with the hope that they might finish with the same record as the Fins and come out on top in the NFL's convoluted tie-breaking scheme. You never want to take your chances in a system that involves such standards as strength of schedule, where your fate is tied to the performance of the teams you've played over the season.

A win against the Titans also would all but eliminate the hated Jets from play-off contention. The Jets had lost to Chicago on Sunday, dropping to a game and a half behind the Pats, two behind the Fins. They couldn't possibly make up two games in two weeks against both the Patriots and Dolphins, not least of all because one team or the other was all but ensured of coming out of the Pats-Dolphins December 29 matchup with a win. If they were to find themselves two games back, the Jets would need to beat the Pats in week 16, hope for a Miami loss to the Vikings, win their own week 17 matchup against the 11–3 Green Bay Packers, then root for the team that they had the better tie-breaker scenario against to stumble in the Pats-Fins game—all for an outside shot at a wild card slot (if a few other AFC contenders managed to slip, too). It would have been simply too much to hope for.

The Monday night matchup also seemed very much like a test of the Pats as a late-season team. New England had been perfect in December a year earlier as they geared up for their run through the play-offs to the Super Bowl. And they were perfect in December again when they arrived in Nashville.

The game we were watching at the Sports Depot felt like the kind of game that would tell us what to expect going forward. It felt like if the Pats beat the Titans, they'd roll on to a second straight AFC East championship and then maybe only the Raiders would stand between them and another Super Bowl appearance. But that was the kind of prognosticating I preferred to leave to fans like Kerrie. I was still approaching the whole thing from a pessimist's point of view.

Bobby probably would have shared my feeling of impending doom if he'd stuck around. But he hadn't stuck around, largely because of his own sense of fatalism.

Bobby, the first person I met at the Sports Depot, had seen enough by the end of the first half. By the time I started talking to Kerrie, he was home, peeking at the game, I'm certain, but refusing to be more thoroughly engaged. He had $100 on the Pats, and it's hard to watch your money slip away from you.

Bobby had gone into the evening hopeful. More than hopeful, really. He went in believing a Pats victory was in the cards. He had taken the Pats getting two points. But he wasn't merely counting on the team to cover; he was counting on them to extend a winning streak that stretched back to their pre-Thanksgiving matchup with the Vikings.

"Three in a row," Bobby said. "That's pretty good. I think they can win four."

"Yeah, but who have they beaten?" I responded. "Tennessee isn't Detroit."

"You're right," he said, a faraway look taking hold of his eyes. "Detroit sucks. But . . . who did they beat last week? Buffalo? Buffalo's pretty good. And they beat them twice."

"Buffalo isn't that good," I responded. "Buffalo isn't Tennessee either."

"They can beat Tennessee," Bobby assured me. "I think they can beat anybody."

And if I hadn't figured it out from the team logo cap he wore over his longish brown hair, I'd have known it then. Bobby was a real Patriots fan. Not a post–Super Bowl party boy late to leap from the bandwagon, but the honest-to-Grogan real deal. Probably had been for most of his 40ish years. So it wasn't like he was faking belief. It wasn't like he was being doggedly optimistic in the face of a torturous season-ending schedule that would make or break the team (and seemed likely to break it). He was simply expressing the honest, heartfelt belief that the Patriots, in spite of all evidence to the contrary, were up to winning any and every game left on their schedule. It struck me that Bobby would have got on famously with Louis from the End Zone.

It wasn't just a good performance from the team that interested Bobby. Nor even a $100 payoff at the end of the night. He was also hoping to score one of the Patriots T-shirts the Sports Depot was giving away. And he wanted a seat at the bar.

Bobby might have found an open bar stool, too, if he'd arrived around the same time I did, 7:30 P.M. The room was fairly full even then, but there was some turnover going on as the remnants of a crowd from some kind of business function slowly dissipated. I was able to get my seat at the very end of the bar right away. And over the half hour that followed, I watched as the self-adhesive name-tag brigade dropped off in twos and threes, replaced by an ever-swelling sea of Bradys, Seymours, and Laws. By the time Bobby showed up around 8:30, Pats fans had more than made up for the departing conventioneers. Every stool was filled.

"I thought I was getting here early enough," Bobby told me, looking around the room and shaking his head. "I could probably get here at six o'clock and not get a seat.

"I don't know if I'll stay," he said. "You can't sit down and watch the Patriots game standing up." Then, recognizing the Berra-ish quality of his statement, he added, "You know what I mean."

He resolved to suck it up, partially, I think, because the Sports Depot was his regular haunt—the bartenders knew him, and they knew his drink (Captain Morgan's and ginger ale)—and partially because he really was hoping to score a free T-shirt (for his girl-friend, he said).

The disappointments just kept coming for Bobby.

He never did get his T-shirt, which had a lot to do with the fact that he never got a seat at the bar. It was also partially my fault, though it's nothing I feel bad about.

I was good about helping Bobby get drinks through the last half hour of the pregame and most of the first half. It was easy. My seat by the taps gave me ready access to the bartenders, and all I had to do was say, "Hey, Bobby needs another," then pass the drink back and some cash forward. (Bobby was a good tipper, which made me like him. Sitting at the bar, I'd noticed that most people tip for shit—a few coins for a round of mixed drinks, like that—but Bobby knew how to take care of the hardworking bar-tenders. That's a sign of a good sort.) But when the time came for the T-shirt giveaway, I had other things on my mind.

It was early in the second quarter when a young woman with curly blonde hair stepped behind the bar with an armful of T-shirts. My attention was focused on the game, which was still scoreless. The Titans had spent the last three and a half minutes of the first quarter and the first half minute of the second moving steadily down the field from their 22 yard line to the Patriots' 23.

"Call her over here," I heard Bobby say from over my left shoulder. "I want to get one of those."

I wanted to tell him there was finally something happening in the game, something potentially big and damaging to the Pats, but my back was turned to him and he never would have heard me unless I turned around. And that would have meant taking my eyes off the TV. So I just kept watching.

"Hey," Bobby shouted at the woman, who stood clear across the bar. "Hey, bring some of those over here."

Titans running back Eddie George dashed through a hole in the right side of the line, picking up 10 yards.

"Hey," Bobby said to me. "Hey, get her to come over here."

Eddie George again. This time for just three yards, to the Patriots' 10 yard line. Second and seven.

"Hey!" Bobby shouted. Out of the corner of my eye, I could see he had his hands up over his head. I thought about telling him he should pay attention to the game, but I decided a guy's gotta determine his own damned priorities.

Richard Seymour broke through the right side to stop George for a one-yard loss, bringing up third and eight at the Pats' 11 yard line.

"You really ought to watch this," I thought as hard as I could. "This is big."

"Hey," Bobby yelled as Tennessee lined up for the third-down play. "Hey, over here."

Titans quarterback Steve McNair broke a tackle and darted the full 11, past the first-down marker and into the end zone to put up the first six points of the game.

The crowd roared gleefully.

I was confused by that reaction for a second. This was the Sports Depot in Allston, Massachusetts, right? Why cheer on Tennessee? Then I took my gaze off the TV and realized the cheer had nothing to do with the touchdown. In fact, almost no one else appeared to have seen the play. They were all clamoring and cheering for free T-shirts. It wasn't all that surprising. A good number of football fans, even fans of defense-focused teams like the Pats, aren't all that interested in D. They want to see pass plays. They want to see their team score. They look at drives by the other team as a chance to grab a beer, take a smoke break, or snag a free T-shirt. Still, I'd have thought a big moment in a big game would have stolen attention away from the giveaways for 15 seconds or so.

It hadn't. Indeed, it hadn't even managed to capture the attention of the guy with a hundred bucks riding on the game's outcome.

"Hey, over here," Bobby half yelled, a tone of defeat taking hold of his voice, as the T-shirt woman's last couple of freebies sailed into the crowd at the far end of the bar. If he were aware of the Tennessee touchdown, it didn't mean as much to him as losing the chance to snag a bar freebie.

As Titans kicker Joe Nedney added the extra point, I thought for a second about how I would have had a much easier time than Bobby getting Goldilocks' attention. And I very nearly started to feel bad about letting Bobby down. Then I remembered Bobby wasn't a friend. He was just some guy I'd encountered in a bar. And my only crime was being focused on the football game, which, really, was supposed to be the point of the evening.

With the T-shirt excitement over, the crowd turned back to the game just in time to see the Pats' offense mount what looked briefly like a drive that would put the Pats on the board, and perhaps even things up.

Antowain Smith picked up four yards on the first play of the drive. Then Brady and Smith combined on a 35-yard pass play, taking the Patriots into Tennessee territory for just the second time in the game and drawing the bar crowd's undivided attention. A play like that might even have been noticed during the T-shirt frenzy.

The Pats picked up just five yards on their next two plays, though. And as they faced third and five at the Tennessee 38 yard line, you could feel that they'd reached a defining moment in the game. Converting on third down would have edged the team right up to the border of Vinatieri's field goal range. As little as six or seven yards on the ensuing three plays would have all but guaranteed three points. More important, though, another first down would have maintained the momentum of a productive drive, perhaps pushing the Pats to tie things up, maybe even reversing the frustrating flow of the entire game.

Bobby could feel it.

"Big play right here," he intoned in the way you will when watching a game, a way that isn't meant to inform anyone of anything, but that's really just an attempt to dislodge the lump from your chest. "Big, big play."

Bobby was right. It was a big play. Unfortunately, the guy who made it big was Titans defensive end Carlos Hall, who charged through the Patriots' line and logged Tennessee's second sack of the game, pushing New England back to the 45 and forcing a punt.

Ken Walter punted into the Titans' end zone with nine minutes left in the half. Then Tennessee spent most of the rest of the quarter moving from their 20 yard line to the Patriots' end zone. Bobby decided to call it a night right after McNair ran in for a second touchdown, putting Tennessee ahead 14–0 with 37 seconds remaining in the half. It wasn't his night, and he knew it. No sense in standing around T-shirtless for another two hours just to watch his hundred dollars slip away.

The 40ish couple who had been sitting next to me at the bar since five minutes after I walked in watched the Patriots fail to do anything in the remaining half minute of the second quarter. Then they headed out, too. They weren't the only ones who left at half-time, either. It was obvious where the game was going. And it was a work night. Why hang on for nothing?

Bobby would have had his seat if he'd stuck around. But he hadn't, which is just as well, because that's when Kerrie and Jaime sat down.

I might not have noticed Kerrie at all, just as I hadn't really paid attention to the people whose seats she and Jaime got—the TV closest to me was to my right, while those stools were to my left—if it weren't for two drunks. There was a sloppy drunk BU dropout to my right who wouldn't stop yammering about how he's going back to school eventually (he never will) and how he needed to find and thank some waitress named Melissa who gave him extra blue-cheese dressing for his Buffalo wings (very exciting). And then there was the slightly less sloppy drunk woman, a holdover from the function that was breaking up when I came in (Hello her name was Patty), who'd moved into Bobby's spot behind me. Unlike Bobby, Patty didn't ask me to help her get a drink. She shouted her order over my head to the bartender, then, when it came, shoved her way by me to grab her drink and knocked over Kerrie's fresh Bud Light. Beer ran off the bar and directly onto my leg.

"How you doin'?" Patty asked me as I attempted to sop some of the beer out of my jeans with a stack of cocktail napkins. That wasn't the "Oh, I'm sorry" I might have expected if it hadn't been for my previous experience with drunks in bars. It wasn't even the not-so-clever quip you normally expect from a drunk in that situation. And my patience had pretty much run out.

"I've got a pant leg full of beer," I said, glaring up at Patty for a second before getting back to work on my pants. "How do you think I'm doing?"

Patty didn't get the message.

"So what's the score?" she asked.

"Fourteen-nothing."

"Are the Patriots winning?"

"No."

"Really? All this yelling and they're not even winning?"

"Yeah," I snapped. "Imagine that."

Finally, whatever wisdom Patty had acquired in her 45 or so years overrode her inebriation and she backed away. I glanced at Kerrie, who'd just got a replacement beer, and she rolled her eyes as if to confirm that it was Patty, not me, who was the problem.

I'd given up on the cocktail napkins and was trying to figure out a way to keep my beer-soaked jeans raised a quarter inch off my leg when Kerrie made her prediction. After that, I was too fascinated with Kerrie's confident devotion to a team that I thought looked just plain lousy to pay much attention to how my pants were doing.

I asked Kerrie how she could possibly be so certain the Pats were going to come back and win. Her answer was simple: She's a diehard, a lifelong fan who has no ability to do anything but believe in her team.

A Rhode Island native, Kerrie was raised a Pats fan. Her grandfather, a big sports fan, had brought up his five daughters with a love of sports, especially of football. Kerrie's mother had carried the tradition to the next level, becoming such a football fanatic that Kerrie's high school friends were afraid to visit on Sundays during the season. Kerrie said she tried not to take things quite that far herself, but she was passionate nonetheless, about the Pats, the Sox, and the Celtics.

"Not the Bs?" I asked.

"Mmmm, I don't know," Kerrie said. "You know. Hockey."

I did know. Hockey is fun to watch live. On TV, not so much. You can never really see the puck. And no one ever scores, mostly.

So it's just kind of impossible to care about hockey unless you love it.

Kerrie and Jaime were roommates at the University of Maryland. Now they were both living in Cambridge. Jaime liked going out to watch games with Kerrie even though she wasn't really a Pats fan.

"She wants to be a Patriots fan," Kerrie told me. "But she isn't a diehard."

Then she whispered, "Really, I think she's a Redskins fan."

I wasn't sure if Kerrie thought that was a bad thing because the Redskins were having such a terrible season or because she was one of those people who thinks you ought to be a fan of the home team.

Kerrie and I kept chatting as the Titans mounted their next offensive drive, but we chatted the way you're supposed to chat when you're a fan watching a game. Kerrie was like me, the kind of person who knows how to talk and watch at the same time. She could pause midsentence to yell at the TV—"Get him! Get him!" as George struggled to get out around the right side—then pick up right where she'd left off. She was the kind of fan you want to be sitting with during a big game. She would never have given a damn about a free T-shirt.

I wanted to know if she had any larger predictions—about the way the rest of the season might go.

"You think they're gonna win this game," I said. "What about after this? Are they gonna make the play-offs? Get back to the Super Bowl?"

"No," Kerrie said, quietly, as we watched Troy Brown fair catch a Titans' punt at the Patriots' 11 yard line. "I don't think so. I'd love for them to go back to the Super Bowl. But it's not gonna happen."

She predicted a Raiders-Eagles Super Bowl. I told her I was thinking either that or Raiders-Packers.

"Where are you from?" she asked me.

"Well, I live in Northampton, but I grew up in Milford, Mass."

"Then you must be a Pats fan," she offered.

"Actually, I'm a Raiders fan."

"Oh," Kerrie said. "That's too bad."

I didn't take offense. I knew exactly what she meant: too bad I didn't have the guts to stick by the home team. Any lifelong Pats fan over the age of 20 has met at least a few dozen guys like me. They know my type. We can't believe. And that probably is too bad.

At least on this night, though, Kerrie probably shouldn't have believed so thoroughly herself. No matter what she predicted, no matter how accurate she'd been in the past, the Patriots were never going to beat the Titans. And they didn't.

On the first play after Brown's fair catch, Brady put the ball in the hands of Titans defensive back Rich Coady, who carried it 24 yards for a touchdown. Brady was sacked for a loss of a yard on the first play of the possession after that. The Pats moved the ball all of eight yards on the next two plays, then punted away to Tennessee. And so most of the rest of the game went. Tennessee padded its lead by three points five minutes into the fourth quarter, then just settled in to grind out most of the rest of the game with clock-munching, run-centered drives.

"That sucks," Kerrie offered as the final seconds ticked off the clock with the Titans up 24–7. She recalled her prediction from early in the half. "Last time I predicted the same thing, and they won. It's probably because you heard me."

"Sorry to be a jinx," I responded. Kerrie offered no relief.

"I think they'll still win the division," I said, attempting to be conciliatory.

"Yeah, they'll win the division," Kerrie agreed. Then she revived her other, less optimistic prediction from earlier in the evening. "But I don't think they're going to the Super Bowl again."

Maybe it was just the disappointment of the evening speaking. Or maybe even a diehard has her limits.

As I put my coat on and told Kerrie I'd enjoyed meeting her, Patty approached us. I thought maybe we were going to get an apology for the spilled beer. I was wrong.

Patty wanted to know if we thought a minihelmet signed by Kevin Faulk might be worth anything.

I refused to acknowledge Patty's presence.

Kerrie simply offered a sharp "I don't know" before turning to say something to Jaime. I wasn't sure whether the tone of her response to Patty was a result of frustration over the outcome of the game, general intolerance for drunken fools, or a lingering anger about the unexpiated beer dumping. Whatever it was, it worked. Patty shuffled away.

When Kerrie turned back to me half a second later, I simply rolled my eyes.

I said good night, shook Kerrie's hand, and Jaime's, and headed out to my car. The painfully frigid mid-December night made me aware again of how wet my pant leg still was. And I worried a bit about what I'd say to the state trooper who was certain to pull me over on my way home. ("It was this drunk named Patty, trooper. I swear. She spilled a beer all over me. You can ask Kerrie." I was pretty sure that wouldn't work.)

I turned on the radio figuring I'd listen to the Patriots' postgame show, but then I thought better of it. I put in a Kinks CD, *Lola vs. Powerman*, instead, and headed for the Pike, yelling over the music for the heat to come on and knowing that, statey or none, it was going to be a long, long drive home.

15.

Game 15 vs. New York Jets

Sunday, December 22, 2002
Record 8–6

Let's start with the Sea-Monkeys. And the Raiders game. And not just because those things came first. But because they were the only two highlights of the day, the only things that went my way. And because everything else was scary, annoying, disappointing, or depressingly entropic. Everything.

I picked up the Amazing Live Sea-Monkeys' MagiQuarium at Hammett's Learning World right after I got to the Natick Mall. That was at about 5:30 P.M.

I parked in the garage outside Macy's, because that was the first garage that came up and I'm way too freaked out by the size of the Natick Mall to go searching for anything else. Then I shoved my way through a dense crowd of last-minute Christmas shoppers, pushing a good three-quarters of the way through the mall to Hammett's, and snagged one of the last three MagiQuariums left on the shelf. That felt good. The Sea-Monkeys weren't really all that important in the grand scheme of things, just a gag stocking-stuffer gift for my wife. But the gag was one I'd been wanting to pull off for most of a month. So the purchase had a sort of artificial bigness about it.

Under normal circumstances, that would have been it for me and the last weekend day before Christmas in retail hell. I'd have weaved my way back through the crowded mall, zipped through Macy's, broken back out to the garage, stopped to breathe a sigh of monoxide-flavored relief, and headed straight for the westbound side of the Mass Pike.

But these weren't normal circumstances, so I didn't just escape the mall. I headed off to Sears to watch some TV.

That, as it turned out, was a mistake.

It wasn't the mall's fault, really. It was just a matter of an error in judgment on my part. But the general discomfort I feel in a place like the Natick Mall at Christmastime certainly didn't help.

I grew up going to the Natick Mall, which has been a major element of the consumerist mecca of Boston's outer western suburbs for as long as I can remember. Together with Shoppers' World (the first shopping mall ever built—now razed and replaced by an endless and unapproachable assemblage of big-box retailers), it forms the center of one of the busiest stretches of an absurdly overdeveloped retail corridor that covers most of the 40 miles of Route 9 between Worcester and Boston.

The Shoppers' World–Natick Mall campus, which straddles the Framingham-Natick line, is flanked by smaller shopping centers and strip malls across Route 9 on one side and Route 30 on the other. There's a multiplex cinema on Flutie Pass, the mall connector road cleverly named for Doug Flutie—the Natick native who was a star quarterback at Boston College, washed out with the Chicago Bears and the Patriots, became the Joe Montana of the Canadian Football League, and returned to the NFL where's he's played the part of the league's most consistently overrated backup QB in stints with Buffalo and San Diego. And stretching out in every possible direction, there's a sea of chain restaurants, ridiculously large furniture outlets, home improvement stores, and discount warehouses. The area around the mall is home to nearly every single thing that's wrong with America, which, of course, makes it mostly irresistible. And entirely intimidating. Especially in the last days before Christmas.

The Natick Mall was pretty big when I was growing up. But it was nothing compared to the supermalls that have become the standard in recent years—and nothing compared to what the Natick Mall itself grew into through a huge expansion project a decade or so ago.

I live a good 100 miles away now. And the mall as it currently exists is unfamiliar to me, and far too big for my taste. So I avoid it as much as I can. But, more often than I'd like, I can't.

There's no Crate & Barrel where I live. No Macy's, either. Nor a Hammett's Learning World, for that matter. And while I hate myself for it, I'm a consumer just like everyone else. So there are times when it becomes necessary to make the trek east to Natick.

My wife and I took a trip out the weekend after Thanksgiving to get some Christmas shopping done—a last bit of it for my wife, the long-term planner in the family, and an initial run for me. She'd spotted the MagiQuarium while we were in Hammett's and joked about how it was all she really wanted for Christmas. The woman ought to know by now that my sense of humor requires me to follow up on such statements, even when—probably particularly when—I know they're not meant to be taken seriously.

I tried addressing the matter close to home. I looked for Sea-Monkeys everywhere I went in the weeks that followed. But I had no success. And in my determination to find the MagiQuarium at some local store, I'd missed my chance to order it online. So with a matter of days remaining between me and the holiday, I'd been left with two choices: forget about my little joke or venture on out to Natick. There was never really a question about what I'd do. Ridiculous obsessions are one of my neurotic specialties.

Originally, I figured I'd complete my errand on Saturday afternoon. Shoot out, hold my breath and muscle my way through the mall, grab the Sea-Monkeys, and get on the Pike as quickly as my car would move. But then I got to thinking—in defiance of everything experience, gut instinct, and plain old common sense told me—that maybe the mall actually was the place to be on Sunday. Maybe, I thought, a big department store's TV section would be the right place to watch the Patriots-Jets game.

This is the way it was supposed to work (the way it actually did work in my imagination):

After capturing a menagerie of playful and smartly attired little Sea-Monkeys, I'd head over to Sears, where I'd set up camp in the TV department. There'd be a whole wall of display-model TVs and at least one free-standing big screen, all, or at least most, of them tuned to the game. I'd tell the salespeople no, I didn't need help; I was just killing time while my wife did some shopping.

I'd hang around the department, watching the game and jawing with the contingent of the late-shopping crowd who'd procrastinated themselves out of a chance to watch what might be the most important game of the Patriots' season. They'd swing by to watch a few plays, or just check on the score, and I'd be the guy they'd ask how things were going. I'd hang with a 40-something fella in a Sox cap for 10 minutes before he went off in search of the perfume his wife likes—he wouldn't know its name, but he'd be pretty sure he could identify it by smell and he'd be almost certain it came in a black bottle—then I'd snicker and scribble snide comments in my notebook as he hustled away. I'd spend half an hour watching and chatting with a college-aged guy in shorts and no coat who'd told his girlfriend he was off to find a men's room, laughing silently every time I caught him glancing nervously over his shoulder. I'd offer a score update to a couple my age, both dressed in team gear, who'd stop by looking tired, sad, and a little bewildered. And I'd actually feel bad for them.

That was the fantasy.

The reality was that Sears didn't have a giant wall of TVs for me to watch. They had a cramped little TV department with a few sets on the back wall and a bunch more on shelves in a couple of narrow aisles. The sets on the wall were showing figure skating and some old Technicolor movie I didn't recognize. But the ones in the aisles were showing the four o'clock games, including the Raiders-Broncos matchup, so I figured the gap between fantasy and reality was still mostly manageable.

With my Sea-Monkeys in hand, I stood in the TV department—moving from one narrow aisle to the next to stay out of the way of the actual customers—and watched the silver-and-black clinch their third-straight AFC West championship.

The Raiders' victory was like an early Christmas gift for me. I needed my team to get to Super Bowl XXXVII. And sewing up their division was a big step in the right direction. Oakland had been denied trips to the Super Bowl under painful circumstances in each of the previous two seasons—in 2000–01, when Baltimore's big, fat asshole of a nose tackle Tony Siragusa belly flopped on top of Rich Gannon, knocking the star QB out of the AFC championship and ensuring his team a win (however cheap) and a trip to Super Bowl XXXV in the process; and in 2001–02 with the famous snow job game in Foxborough. And it appeared the Raiders would have just one more chance at a Lombardi trophy before salary-cap restrictions and age conspired to rob the team of some of its best players. It appeared unlikely at the time that Gannon, Jerry Rice, and Tim Brown would all be around for another season. So they had to get it done, and winning the West was an essential part of the push.

Other than a Sears salesman, no one asked me about the Raiders game, but a good number of people stopped by to take a peek. That seemed like a pretty good sign to me. At the very least, it confirmed that there were people in the mall who were interested in keeping up with football scores.

Of course, the Raiders-Broncos game had absolutely no bearing on the Patriots. It wouldn't have even if the Broncos had been in the hunt for a wild card spot, which they weren't.

It was clear that there would be no wild card teams coming out of the AFC East. (It was still mathematically possible for a team from the East to grab a wild card spot, but the trends made it clear that wasn't going to happen.) So with the end of the regular season, the division champions would advance while the other three AFC East teams would start planning for the 2003 season.

And Miami's Saturday afternoon loss to the hapless Minnesota Vikings had put the Patriots back in control of their play-off destiny. Going into their game with the Jets, the Pats, at 8–6, were half a game behind the 9–6 Dolphins. Beating the 7–7 Jets and going on to beat the Dolphins in week 17 would give New England the division crown. A loss to the Jets wouldn't eliminate the Pats, but it would make things way more complicated. They'd need to beat Miami and hope for a Jets loss to Green Bay.

And while a Raiders victory did put Oakland a step closer to securing home-field advantage through the play-offs, that was little more than a minor concern to the Pats. Whichever team won the East was going to have to win some road games to get to the Super Bowl. Where those games would be played was far less important than what team would be playing them.

The mere fact that people were coming by to check scores made me feel like things were going mostly according to plan.

Somewhere out in the crowded mall, that guy in the Sox cap was picking up an electronic golf score keeper for his brother-in-law in Florida and realizing he wasn't gonna make it home by kickoff. Somewhere that couple in the Pats gear was discussing whether a bonsai tree would make a good gift for his boss and not even thinking about the fact that they were burning daylight.

But as the day wound on and the Raiders moved closer to victory, the crowd in Sears started to dwindle. Customers stopped pushing by me in the tight aisles. Idle salespeople made more and more passes by me. And by the time the game headed for its conclusion (28–16 Raiders), there was almost no one other than me and the sales staff left in the TV department.

A young saleswoman came by, stopped for a moment, then stepped just behind me and craned to look over my shoulder as I jotted some notes. I assume she thought I was taking down prices. Another saleswoman, this one middle-aged, stared at me from her post in the appliances department until all I could do was stare back and wonder if her hair color (dark brown going on black) was natural. A mid-50s-ish guy in a blue sport coat stopped briefly in the aisle between electronics and appliances and gave me the stink eye.

I decided it was time to take a little cruise around the mall to size up the likelihood that things would get better. It turned out that they probably wouldn't.

The crowds that had vexed me endlessly just a few hours earlier as I'd pushed through the mall from Macy's to Hammett's and on to Sears were all but gone. I moved easily through the mall, first looping around the upper level, then the lower, hoping to catch a glimpse of the guy in the Sox cap or the kid in the shorts. Nothing. I moved back through Macy's and stepped out into the garage, where the main thrust of traffic was outward.

The department store plan clearly wasn't going to work. Unless I wanted to watch the game surrounded by an assortment of alternatingly hopeful and suspicious salespeople. And that wasn't anything like what I'd imagined. So I decided I'd better find a bar somewhere.

* * *

I had my pick of chain restaurant lounges. Or at least the ones with TVs. I was pretty sure the Pizzeria Uno across Route 9 had no TV at its bar. I thought maybe the Chili's just down the road did, but I wasn't sure. I knew for sure, though, that I could watch the game at the Chi-Chi's restaurant on Route 30 in Framingham, just on the other side of Shoppers' World. I'd seen a lot of games there back when I was still living in the area.

I remembered sitting with a table full of friends at Margaritaville, which is what Chi-Chi's calls its lounge, watching Larry Bird lead the Celtics to victory. Margaritaville was a pretty lively place to watch a game back then—large and always fairly full, with a pair of big-screen sets and a handful of smaller ones scattered through the place. You never had to worry about where you sat; you could always see the game. So I decided Margaritaville had to be my best bet.

As I pulled into a parking lot that wasn't jammed but was full enough to make me feel confident, I worried briefly about the potential negative effects of leaving the Sea-Monkeys ("actually a species of brine shrimp"), even in their freeze-dried state, sitting in my car. It wasn't a terrible evening weatherwise, but there's never anything warm about a late-December night in New England and I had no idea whether the freezing temperatures posed a threat to the future inhabitants of the MagiQuarium.

I scanned the box for information, but learned only that the manufacturer, ExploraToy, absolutely guarantees the little guys to live "up to two whole years." That and the fact that the illustrations on the box are "fanciful." I wasn't sure what the Sea-Monkeys might spend their two years in the MagiQuarium doing, but apparently they wouldn't be wearing sunglasses, throwing dance parties, or riding Razor scooters. I could only hope my wife wouldn't be too heartbroken.

I decided to take my chances with the Sea-Monkeys and their shockingly boring lives and headed into Chi-Chi's on my own.

Margaritaville wasn't quite the place I remembered from more than a decade earlier. Or perhaps it was too much the place I remembered from then. Very little had changed that I wouldn't attribute to decay.

There was still a big-screen TV in one corner and some smaller screens posted above the bar and scattered around the room. Some or all of those sets may have been new—or at least newish. Chi-Chi's had installed a pool table over by the big screen, where some prime lounge tables used to be. And there was some sort of minor construction project taking place over by the far side of the bar. Other than that, it was the same old Margaritaville, only in need of a fresh coat of paint, a new carpet, and perhaps a new bar.

It could also have used a better crowd.

There were a dozen or so Pats fans on hand when I walked in shortly after eight, but they weren't a particularly exciting bunch. In fact, the only one of them who was animated in any way during the half hour leading up to kickoff was an obnoxious jackass who seemed to think he was a wisecracking ESPN studio show host (a far less intelligent Keith Olbermann, maybe, or a far less knowledgeable and clever Chris Berman).

He was already into his act—and obviously three sheets to the wind—when I walked in and perched on a stool in the middle of one side of the square bar. He sat at the corner of the bar to my right with a trio of buddies, participating in ESPN's highlight show, *NFL Primetime,* loudly and ignorantly, much to the amusement of his friends.

"Bam!" he yelled cleverly on seeing a big hit from the New York Giants–Indianapolis Colts game. "That's my booooy!" he offered with irresistible wit as Giants running back Tiki Barber plunged in for a touchdown.

On watching a player's helmet pop off after a powerful hit in the Green Bay–Buffalo game, one of his buddies posed, "What's it gotta feel like to get your helmet ripped off?"

The anti-Olbermann's response: "Not good, Danny. Not good."

If I'd been in the mood to be generous (like in the holiday spirit or something), I might have assumed his pal's name was Danny. As it was, I could only believe he thought he was talking to Olbermann's former SportsCenter coanchor Dan Patrick.

I grew to hate anti-Olbermann well before the game ever got started. I hated his big, stupid, drunken grin and the plump upper lip at its center. I hated his stupid little round glasses. I hated his rounded stomach and, above it, the pecs that might actually have been man breasts. But most of all I hated his complete inability to shut up.

I got to hating his buddies soon enough, too. They didn't bother me so much at first—the guy in the black T-shirt and the Bud cap, the guy who looked like Meathead from *All in the Family,* and the guy who looked like the Green Arrow from the *Justice League of America*—but that was probably because anti-Olbermann never stopped talking long enough to let them assert their own idiocy.

That changed just before game time when the lot of them got to discussing the suspected homosexuality of another bar patron who'd come in wearing a scarf. (A scarf. Their evidence that the guy was gay was that he was wearing a scarf on December 22.) The bartender, a geeky fellow who needed desperately to do something about the hair on the back of his neck, joined in happily. Their target was across the room, oblivious to the discussion, but I wasn't. And while I was too much of a chicken to say anything to them, I did manage to vent some of my frustration by stiffing the offensive barkeep at the end of the night.

It wasn't long after the game started, though, that my outlook on anti-Olbermann turned a bit. As play got underway and he began inserting himself in the ESPN *Sunday Night Football* crew's color commentary, I found myself taking a bit of pleasure from his failed attempts to establish himself as a football expert.

Four minutes into the first quarter, with the game still scoreless, the Patriots were called for a penalty during a punt.

"That's an illegal block," anti-Olbermann announced smugly.

"He knows it before the TV guys," Green Arrow chimed in.

But it turned out not to be an illegal block.

"It's illegal touching," anti-Olbermann declared.

Wrong again.

"It's offsides."

Strike three.

It turned out to be a procedure call. It pushed the Pats' punting team back five yards. But it didn't push anti-Olbermann out of his imaginary seat in the announcers' booth.

He continued to work as an unofficial color commentator throughout the first half, questioning the play calls, arguing with the ESPN crew, and invariably shouting out "holding" whenever he saw a flag fly in the offensive backfield. I kept thinking one of the guy's buddies should tell him that yelling "holding" every time there's an offensive penalty called is like yelling "blitz" every time you see the safeties advance on the line of scrimmage before the snap; you can't help but be right a good 70 or 80 percent of the time. But all it proves is that you've seen a football game before. The thing is, though, I don't think any of the guy's friends had quite figured that out.

As anti-Olbermann continued his irritating act, he started to turn me against the Patriots in a weird way. He didn't actually make me root for the Jets or anything. It was just that the worse the Pats looked (and at times they looked simply pathetic), the less talking he did. And there were points in the evening at which I simply had more interest in Mr. Obnoxious shutting up than I did in seeing the Patriots win.

When Jets quarterback Chad Pennington hit wide receiver Laveranues Coles for a 32-yard touchdown five minutes into the first quarter, anti-Olbermann had nothing to say. When Kevin Faulk returned the ensuing kickoff for a touchdown to tie the game at seven, anti-Olbermann let out a long, loud "Daaaaaaaaaaaamn!" When Pennington completed another touchdown pass to wide receiver Santana Moss late in the quarter, there wasn't so much as a groan from the corner of the bar. When Adam Vinatieri nailed a 49-yard field goal early in the second quarter, I had to endure a booming "Iiiiiiiiiiiiiiiiiiiiit's good!"

Anti-Olbermann's doofus friends continued to find their pal's comments pithy. Me, not so much.

It's possible that none of it would have bothered me quite so much if the Pats had played a better game. Or if they'd simply looked like they had some interest in winning the game—if they'd played as if they were involved in a vital contest against a major rival that was competing with them for the division championship and a play-off berth.

But the Pats never looked for so much as a minute like the game mattered to them. They came out looking flat—going three and out on their first two offensive possessions and earning only one first down in the entire first quarter—and continued to look flat throughout the game, except during one stellar drive at the beginning of the third quarter. The Jets, on the other hand, looked like champions. They bested the Pats in virtually every aspect of the game.

And even after that big Pats drive, which tied the score at 17–17, it was obvious New England was on its way to a second straight prime-time loss. Worse yet, that loss was going to take control of the division race away from the Pats and give it back to Miami. For the Patriots to win the AFC East, they'd not only need to beat Miami in week 17, but also for the Jets to lose to Green Bay. And while the Packers were undoubtedly a great team, they were also a team whose play-off berth was secured; they'd be playing for the top seeding in the NFC when they got to the Meadowlands, but that's not nearly as big a motivator as playing to make the postseason. If the Jets and Pats both won, New York's better division record than the Dolphins' and better record against common opponents than the Pats' would give them the tie-breaker and hand them the division. Only Miami would go into the final week of the season with the ability to win the East by winning its game.

I wasn't the only one in the bar who could see where things were headed.

Anti-Olbermann took off his imaginary headset and headed for the door late in the third with the game still tied and the Jets driving toward what would end up being a field goal. I went back to rooting for the Pats, but it didn't matter. New England put in minimal effort, got minimal results, and walked away with a 30–17 loss.

And even though the Pats technically were still in the hunt for the division title, by the end of the game it had become clear that Pats fans couldn't expect much good to come out of week 17. If the team didn't find a way to lose, Green Bay would.

It was obvious that any lingering notions about the Patriots being play-off contenders could only be fanciful. The Pats were no more likely to see action in January than the Sea-Monkeys were to join the circus. I wasn't sure what the Pats might end up doing during the five weeks ahead, but clearly it wouldn't involve winning a second straight AFC East title or getting back to the Super Bowl. I could only hope Pats fans wouldn't be too heartbroken.

I realized I had lost my ability to believe. I rejoined the Sea-Monkeys in my car and we headed west—away from Margaritaville and anti-Olbermann, away from the other chain restaurants and the malls, away from the idle salespeople and the too-small TV department, and most of all, away from the Patriots—as fast as we could go without getting in trouble.

16.

Game 16 vs. Miami Dolphins

Sunday, December 29, 2002
Record 8–7

There were never 68,000 fans in Gillette Stadium this after-noon. There might have been 60,000 at one point, but that's about it. There have been empty seats in patches and chunks throughout the stadium since kickoff. There are seats, even now, that remain covered with snow. No one ever needed to use them, so no one ever cleared them off.

There are far fewer of us here now than there were half an hour ago, too. Far, far fewer than there were when the Patriots fell 11 points behind the Miami Dolphins with five minutes left to play in the game.

Those of us who remain are loud, though. We're excited. And we're happy.

We are the fortunate, the wise, and the faithful. Some of us are probably plain old gluttons for punishment. Others were just too drunk or too stunned to walk away when all seemed lost. And many of us are simply too stubborn not to stick things out to the bitter end.

Whatever our individual reasons, we're all still here, watching and cheering as the Patriots once again stand positioned to accom-plish the improbable (not long ago I would have said inconceiv-able): an overtime win against a Dolphins team that dominated the Pats for most of this last game of the regular season and seemed to have the match—and the AFC East title—sewn up two-thirds of the way through the fourth quarter.

It's as hard as ever to gauge depth from my seat here in the far end zone. The Patriots, who tied the game playing toward me, now are moving in the opposite direction, headed toward the Route 1 side of the stadium. They're marching toward the Miami end zone, I know that, but it's hard to get a grip on exactly how close they are without help from the scoreboard.

It's not just me. Depth-perception issues are a well-established drawback of end zone seats. Football is a game best viewed laterally. You just can't see a yard—or five, or even 10 sometimes—when you're looking straight at it. This is why televised football games are photographed from the sides or from above. And the closer you get to the field sitting in the end zone, the more difficult it becomes to assess distance. As the action moves away from you, and the angle of your line of sight diminishes, it gets harder and harder to distinguish one yard from several.

I'm low. Row 15 of section 122. It's about as close to the field as I've ever been for a professional football game. And I've been hearing expressions of puzzlement over depth issues throughout the game.

Early in the first quarter, as the Pats began a drive from the Miami 39 yard line, moving toward my end zone, Tom Brady completed a pass to David Patten.

"Three yards," a woman two rows in front of me exclaimed excitedly.

More like five, it seemed to me.

"It's eight," came a cry from a few rows behind me.

I thought, hey, the guy might be right.

Then the scoreboard told us it was second down and four. The gain on the reception, then, was six. No one in section 122 was about to argue.

Later in the same quarter, the Pats began a drive from their own 32 yard line. The fans around me cheered mightily as Brady hit Kevin Faulk for what looked like a nice little pickup. Then the scoreboard informed us it was second and nine.

"One yard?" asked a lone voice from behind me. One yard it was.

No one else expressed any kind of shock. By then, most of us had realized it was hopeless to try to get a real read of yardage from our vantage point.

* * *

And now all we can do is check the scoreboard between plays. The Pats started this opening drive of overtime at their own 40 after Miami's Olindo Mare kicked off out of bounds. It appeared that mistake was about to cost the Dolphins dearly.

Although the Pats failed to make anything of a trick play on their first play of the drive—Tom Brady lateraled to Patten, who then attempted a pass to Troy Brown—they got about moving the ball downfield fairly quickly thereafter. A 15-yard pickup by Faulk on an end-around got them into Miami territory. And another big play involving Faulk, a 20-yard reception, took them to the Miami 25 yard line, well within Adam Vinatieri's field goal range.

The Patriots did little with their next two plays. But then on third and nine Brady completed a pass to Brown that got the ball to the 17. That wasn't enough to get the Pats a new set of downs, but it didn't really matter. Three points would win the game just as well as six. Vinatieri just needed to make a 35-yard kick to put those points on the board.

So now Vinatieri is trotting onto the field. And everyone here in the stadium—not to mention every Pats, Fins, and Jets fan watching at home—knows what happens whenever the super-accurate Pats kicker attempts to win a game from this close.

A group of young guys had filed into the empty row in front of me after abandoning their push to leave the stadium late in the fourth quarter. Now, one of them turns around and looks at me. He's wearing a giant grin. "This is insane," he says.

"Yeah," I say before he turns back around to watch the kick. "It's amazing."

We're both right.

There isn't a seat in the stadium that would have afforded any perspective on what has happened here today—or what has happened with the Patriots this year. Sixteen games into New England's post–Super Bowl XXXVI season, there's still no making sense of the defending champs.

This is the team that silenced doubters who claimed its victory over the heavily favored St. Louis Rams in Super Bowl XXXVI was a fluke, a lucky break, by starting its season with a crushing victory over the Pittsburgh Steelers, the team most experts tagged as the favorites to represent the AFC in Super Bowl XXXVII. This is the team that followed that opening Monday night victory with impressive wins over the New York Jets on the road and the Kansas City Chiefs at home, convincing skeptics in New England (including me) and across America in the process. It's also the team that then lost four straight before bouncing back with a big road win at Buffalo. It's the team that staggered to 8–5 heading into the stretch, then dropped big games at Tennessee and at home against the Jets, appearing, in both cases, to have lost the fire that propelled it to its first Super Bowl victory and into the early part of the current season.

And this is the team that came out today with its play-off hopes on the line, knowing it would only make the postseason if it beat Miami and if Green Bay beat the Jets in their late game in New Jersey. It's the team that entered this game looking hungry and ready to make a run at the postseason, that started with two strong defensive stands and a respectable drive on offense, that appeared to be poised to win a field-position battle. It's the team that then gave up a key fumble and subsequently fell apart, allowing the Dolphins to make their three first-half touchdowns look easy while struggling to find the end zone themselves. It's the team that went into halftime looking like its season was over, down 21–10 and apparently outclassed by Miami.

And for most of the second half, things went about the same. Miami didn't score until late in the fourth quarter, but it didn't need to. It was moving the ball effectively on virtually every drive, keeping the clock running and protecting its lead. And the Pats were sputtering.

The fans in section 122 weren't shy about expressing their disdain during the 33 minutes of regulation play in which the Pats insisted on playing poorly.

The pair of tobacco-chewing 20-year-olds sitting immediately to my left were among the first to express their issues with any real volume. Three and a half minutes into the second quarter, with Miami leading 7–0, Ricky Williams broke out around the right end for a 16-yard pickup, taking the Fins to the Patriots' 32 yard line and bringing Williams' rushing total for the game up to a frightening 63 yards.

"Will you stop the run?" the kid farthest from me yelled, his exasperation as visible as his breath. "Jesus!"

The Pats didn't comply. Two and a half minutes later, Williams went around the right end yet again and carried the ball 14 yards into the end zone.

Dipper #2 spun around and punched the back of his seat. "These guys fuckin' suck!" he shouted.

The dippers cheered loudly along with the rest of the crowd when Antowain Smith put the Pats on the board with an 11-yard touchdown run late in the half. But they were back on New England's case pretty much immediately, as the Dolphins drove 76 yards in just six plays, including a 30-yard Williams run and a 32-yard touchdown pass from Jay Fiedler to wide receiver James McKnight.

"This is unreal," Dipper #1 offered as McKnight's catch put the Fins back on top by two scores. "Our defense sucks."

Others joined in as the game wore on.

When the Pats started the third quarter with a three-play drive that produced all of two yards, the goateed guy to my right hollered out through his mouthful of sunflower seeds, "Way to come out strong in the third, boys. Whooo-hoo!" Dipper #1 just buried his face in his hands, muttering, "Way to go, champs."

Things got worse from there.

Five minutes into the third, with Miami ahead 21–10 and Williams moving the ball successfully on play after play (five yards here, another nine there), the middle-aged men with the Rhode Island accents sitting just behind me started talking about what was wrong with the Pats. One of them, a guy with a gray-brown beard and a collection of lift tickets dangling from his green ski parka, sussed it out this way: "Their defensive line sucks. Their offensive line sucks. Their running backs suck." He paused for a few seconds, then, "They could use another cornerback, too." And except for the fact that one of the Pats running backs, Faulk, was having a half-decent day, there was little in what he said that anyone could argue with.

Once again, I thought about Louis from the End Zone. I wondered if even he would be able to blame me or my neighbors in section 122 for our inability to believe in the Pats.

New England's prospects started looking slightly more solid when Vinatieri hit from 36 yards out late in the third to make it 21–13, but even then there didn't seem to be any real hope for a Patriots comeback. The way they'd been playing it was clear that they just didn't have the stuff.

As Miami lined up to start a drive with 9:45 remaining in the fourth quarter, Pats defensive players lifted their arms, signaling for the fans, who'd fallen quiet, to get into the game. We gave them what they were looking for, rising to our feet and cheering loudly.

"They'd better earn it," one of the Rhode Island guys offered.

And for the first time since the beginning of the first quarter, the D did earn the crowd's support, forcing a punt after just three plays. But on the first play after the punt, Brady threw an interception. And three minutes of game time later, Mare hit a 28-yard field goal that put Miami ahead 24–13 with 4:59 remaining in the game.

"It would have been a hell of a comeback," Dipper #2 said as he turned to head for the gates. "That's the straw," Dipper #1 offered as he trailed his buddy out of row 15. "That's the straw."

"See you all next year," a woman in a Troy Brown game jersey offered as she filed out. She struck me as just a little too cheery. But maybe it was just that she'd accepted the inevitability of a Pats loss and moved on.

Throughout the stadium, lines formed on the stairways. It was over. The Pats were on their way to completing the season with an exact reversal of the way they began it, dropping three straight games to key opponents. An up-and-down season as defending league champs was wrapping up depressingly deep on the down side. And, at least for the moment, believers were in extremely short supply.

Only, it wasn't really over after all. With everything apparently lost, the Pats came back to life.

On the drive following the Mare field goal that appeared to cinch things for the Fins, the Patriots moved 68 yards in 10 plays, using just more than two of the five minutes left in the game. They scored on a three-yard pass from Brady to Brown. And then Brady hit Christian Fauria on the two-point conversion. Miami's lead was cut to three.

The kickoff team lined up like they were going to try an on-side kick, but Vinatieri booted the ball deep into Dolphins territory. Return man Travis Minor fielded the kick at the two-yard line and carried it out only as far as the four, putting Fiedler and the offense in a difficult spot.

Then the D that hadn't stopped much of anything through most of the game found its strength. They shut Miami down on its first two plays, then gave up seven on third down. The Fins had to punt from their 11, which would have been bad enough for Miami even if punter Mark Royals hadn't shanked the kick, dumping the ball out of bounds at the Dolphins' 34 yard line.

The crowd that remained in the stadium at that point might have numbered 30,000. Or we might have been fewer. But we cheered like we were 68,000 strong. And the team kept us cheering.

They moved the ball just nine yards in three plays after the punt, but that set Vinatieri up to tie the game from 43 yards out.

After the kick came rocketing through the goalposts toward us, the entirety of section 122 (indeed, the whole end zone) paused for an odd second as if we'd come not just to distrust our depth perception but our ability to tell a field goal from a miss—or maybe we were waiting to see if there would be a flag coming in from somewhere, or a replay showing that the kick had actually gone wide. Then it hit us that the whole thing was real. And we shouted and high-fived and made smart statements like "Holy shit" and "Can you fucking believe this?" to the people around us without thinking about whether they were friends, strangers, or Jehovah's Witnesses.

It didn't matter. Because once again the Pats had swung things around, not just on the field but in the stands. Once again, we were all believers. Every one of us. I looked around for Louis, wanting to give him a thumbs-up, but if he was in the stadium, he was nowhere near section 122.

* * *

The Pats won the overtime coin toss and took charge from there. And now we're all standing, trying hard to be quiet, as Vinatieri lines up to try the game-winner. The ball is snapped, the kick goes up, it hooks dangerously toward the right upright, but it stays just inside the goal posts. Vinatieri has yet again lifted the Pats to dramatic victory.

We turn to our neighbors and high-five and hug. We watch the celebration on the field and the replay on the scoreboard. Then we start to really celebrate. Fans are dancing. Fans are jumping and screaming. The high-fives and hugs continue. A young guy a few rows down from me climbs up onto the back of a couple of chairs, arms raised above his head, and screams at the top of his lungs.

And me, I'm laughing. Just laughing uncontrollably. I can't believe what I've just seen. But I have to believe it. I have no choice. And even though I know it might not matter, even though I'm still aware, somewhere in the back of my head, that there's still a late game at the Meadowlands standing between the Pats and the play-offs, I'm too swept up in the moment to care. I don't remember ever feeling this way about the Patriots. Not after Super Bowl XXXVI. Not after the week 1 win over Pittsburgh. Not ever. I can't explain why, but I believe. I'm not entirely sure what I believe. I just believe. And I decide, without really thinking about it, that if believing ends up kicking my ass in three hours, I can live with that.

The young newcomer in front of me turns around and looks at me again, his grin twice as big as it was in the moment before Vinatieri's second big kick of the game.

"Insane," I say with a nod and a giant grin of my own.

We continue dancing in the stands for maybe 10 minutes, then head for the exits. And our giddy energy persists. It's almost as if the Pats have won the Super Bowl again.

They haven't, of course. Indeed, we all know the Pats can't even make the play-offs unless the Jets lose to Green Bay, but in a lot of ways that doesn't matter. And it's not just the fact that they've eliminated the hated Dolphins that has us buzzing.

The Patriots have finished their season with a winning record. They've remained in contention for a division in which they were projected to finish third. They've pulled a victory out of nowhere yet again and they've completed an up-and-down season very much on the up side.

And best of all, they've proven that this team can have a future. The Patriots' championship season followed one in which they finished 5–11. There's no telling how far they'll go on the heels of a 9–7 year. There's no reason not to be hopeful about the team that will take the field in September. There's no reason to expect the Pats of 2003 will fall flat. And there's every reason to hope they'll be right back in the thick of things. That's not something New England sports fans have often been able to say with confidence. It is now. And right now, for this moment, that's enough.

As we file out of the stadium gates and push our way across Route 1 toward the parking lots, someone yells, "Go Packers!" A cheer runs through the crowd and even I join in.

Then someone with a radio yells out that the Jets have drawn first blood, getting out ahead of the Pack 7–0.

"A touchdown?" a woman walking just ahead of me says. "That's nothing. They'll lose."

A touchdown isn't really nothing, but it can be close to it when your opponent is Green Bay. Brett Favre is still the best quarterback in the league. And his team is playing for the top seed in its conference for a reason.

Still, with all the Pats fans around me, I hear only that one expression of confidence. Everyone else is either scared about how the Jets-Packers game will turn out or too superstitious to say anything about it.

Making my way down Route 1 to the parking lot at the End Zone, where I've left my car once again, I keep my ears open for further shouted updates on the Jets game. But I get none.

I find the game on the radio when I get back to my car, though. And I'm not even halfway home before it becomes obvious that the Pack isn't going to be able to give the Patriots a hand. The Jets are on a mission. They end up winning 42–17, capturing the AFC East crown in the process. In the end, the Jets owe the Pats a debt of gratitude; by taking down the Dolphins, New England has cleared the Jets' path to the postseason.

By the time I reach Exit 4 and start the last leg of my last trip home from a Pats game this season, I've started thinking about the Raiders and what might be their final chance to get to the Super Bowl for at least a few years to come. With the Patriots eliminated, I can start focusing on being an Oakland fan full time again. That feels good. It feels like it's coming just in time. But it also feels kind of strange.

I don't know whether I'll still be a Patriots believer when September rolls around. I don't even know why I remain a believer now, with New England eliminated from the play-offs all because they couldn't find it in them to win one or two vital games. But I do still believe. And I find myself looking forward to next season even while I know that, for me and my chosen team, this season still has as many as four weeks left in it.

It's hard to understand. And the more I think about it, and the farther the events of the day, and of the entire season, move away from me, the more difficult it is to achieve any kind of perspective. So I decide to stop trying and just let things go as they will. I latch on to the good feeling for a change. And I let it carry me the rest of the way home.

Epilogue

"Twenty-four to ten."

I said it as if it were an absolute certainty, as if Super Bowl XXXVIII had already happened. In truth, the game was still four days away.

"Really?" Gainer asked.

"Absolutely," I offered without a second's hesitation. "It's gonna be a blowout."

"I don't know," Gainer came back. "Obviously, I think the Patriots are gonna win. But I can't see a blowout."

"I can," I said. "Here's why: Super Bowls are always the opposite of what everyone thinks they're going to be. Everyone thinks this one's gonna be close. So that means it has to be a blowout. And the Panthers sure as hell aren't blowing out the Pats."

"I'll give you that," Gainer said. "But I still don't think we're gonna get a blowout. I'm thinking the Patriots by three."

"Nah," I said, dangerously sure of myself. "Blowout. Watch."

Gainer was right. The Patriots beat the Carolina Panthers in Super Bowl XXXVIII by three points, 32–29, winning the NFL championship for the second time in three years, and doing it, once again, with an Adam Vinatieri field goal at the end of regulation play.

But in the end, I didn't mind being wrong about the final score. All I cared about was the fact that the Pats had grabbed another Lombardi trophy. They'd rebounded brilliantly from their disappointing finish in 2002. More than brilliantly, in fact. Super Bowl XXXVIII marked the Patriots' 15th straight win. Theirs was the second-longest single-season winning streak in NFL history (after the 17-game streak posted by the Miami Dolphins in their undefeated 1972 season). More important, in winning the Super Bowl a second time, the Pats had proven—to their fans, to the football-watching world, and to me—that the 2001–02 season hadn't been a fluke; it had, it was clear, marked the start of an unequaled period in Patriots history, a period in which the team will be taken seriously, will be viewed as a real NFL powerhouse, will be expected to make the play-offs most years, and will be viewed as a legitimate contender for the league championship when it does reach the postseason. The Patriots of my youth were not only dead, but securely, thoroughly, inexhumably buried.

And what was truly strange about all of it for me was the fact that somewhere in the midst of everything, I had come around to believing. Really believing in the New England Patriots. I hadn't simply become convinced that the Patriots were destined to win Super Bowl XXXVIII in the two weeks between the conference championship games and the Super Bowl. It wasn't a belief specific to a single game or a single opponent. I had been certain that the Pats were headed for a second Lombardi trophy since sometime in late November. I had become certain that no team in the AFC could beat the Pats—and since no NFC team was going to beat any of the top six AFC teams in the Super Bowl, that meant a championship was in the cards for New England.

I hadn't become a Patriots fan for real. But that's only to say that the Pats hadn't taken the Raiders' place in my heart. I had, however, become more like a Patriots fan than I'd ever been in my life. Once a distant second favorite to my Raiders, the Pats had closed the gap to within inches.

And it felt good.

It started sinking in just as the Patriots started to heat up again. October 5. Five weeks into football season, with the Pats at 2–2 on the season and the Tennessee Titans visiting Foxborough.

It might have hit sooner if I'd had time to pay attention to football. But I hadn't. My son, Seamus, was born in late September, and I hadn't seen a game in either of the two weekends that followed his birth.

I had seen the Pats take a beating in the season opener, losing 31–0 to the Bills in Buffalo. And I'd watched them rebound a week later, rolling over the Philadelphia Eagles 31–10 on the road. And I knew from the papers that the games that followed had produced a 23–17 home victory over the Chad Pennington–less New

York Jets and a 20–17 road loss to the then-hot Washington Red-skins. So it looked to me as if the Pats were off to what would be yet another frustrating season. A win here, a loss there. Another 9–7 finish, maybe. Or 10–6 if they got really lucky. Nothing terri-ble. Nothing spectacular.

My Raiders were also 2–2 heading into that weekend, though their two wins hadn't been nearly so encouraging as the Pats'. The Raiders, who had made it to Super Bowl XXXVII only to be clob-bered by the Tampa Bay Buccaneers 48–21, had started their season with losses to the Titans and Denver Broncos and wins over peren-nial pushovers the Cincinnati Bengals and San Diego Chargers.

I didn't have high hopes for either team, which meant I wasn't expecting much out of the season. I might have been depressed by the whole thing if I hadn't had something far more important to feel joyful about. As it happened, I just kind of resigned myself to not paying all that much attention. I knew I'd get back to watching at some point—because football was still football—but I wasn't in any kind of a hurry. Or at least I wasn't through Saturday evening.

Then Sunday morning rolled around. And I started thinking about football at about the same time I started thinking about my lawn. Right around 11 o'clock.

The lawn hadn't been on my mind any more than the NFL over the preceding two weeks. But the grass hadn't stopped grow-ing. And fall hadn't stopped threatening to come on. So I knew I was going to have to get out into the yard and knock the lawn down if I didn't want to end up, a week or two later, struggling to rake leaves out of a tangle of overgrown grass.

I put my work boots on, rolled the mower out into the unsea-sonably warm late morning, and, without conscious contempla-tion, hopped into my car. I needed to go buy a portable radio. Im-mediately. I needed to catch the Pats' game.

While there was no way I was going to see a one o'clock game and get the lawn mowed, I was damned if I wasn't at least going to hear the Pats-Titans match.

I grabbed the cheapest AM/FM Walkman-type radio I could find at the CVS down the street and boogied back home excited about the Patriots. And confident that a win was in the offing.

* * *

It's not like there was no reason to feel good about the Pats' chances that day. After all, New England had beaten Tennessee five of the six times the teams had met in Foxborough. And the Pats' 2–2 record wasn't far off the Titans' 3–1.

Still, there was the memory of the humiliating 24–7 Monday night loss in Tennessee that had all but ended the Pats' 2002 season. And there was the fact that the Titans had been tagged by a number of experts as a leading contender to represent the AFC in Super Bowl XXXVIII. The Pats weren't even favored to win their division.

There's always a reason to hope for a win. But there was next to no reason for any Patriots fan to expect one that afternoon. There was even less reason for a Raiders fan and sworn Patriots nonbeliever to expect a Pats' win.

But I did expect a win. And as the game played out—and the lead switched back and forth—I never stopped expecting one.

I gave a bag full of grass cuttings a vigorous shakeout in the woods behind my house in celebration of the 58-yard pass from Tom Brady to Troy Brown that tied the game at six late in the first quarter (Vinatieri then made it a 7–6 Pats' lead). I turned the mower off to listen to the call of a one-yard rush by Antowain Smith that made it 14–13 in the Patriots' favor early in the third. When Mike Cloud darted in from the one yard line to put the Pats up 21–16 at the end of the third, my wild screaming scared the bejesus out of a neighbor, who probably thought I'd got my arm caught in the mower. I rushed into the house to watch what might have been a go-ahead drive by Tennessee late in the fourth. And I celebrated—quietly, so as not to wake the baby—when Ty Law intercepted Steve McNair and went 65 yards to score a touchdown and put the Pats ahead 38–27. Then I went back outside to put the mower away, thinking the Patriots might be better than I'd believed.

As it turned out, that was the least of it. The 2003–04 Pats ended up being better than anyone had expected.

The win over the Titans began what would be a 12-game winning streak to end the regular season. The Pats finished with the best record in franchise history, 14–2. They entered the 2004 play-offs as the top seed in the AFC for the first time ever. They beat the Titans again in the second round of the play-offs (as the

number-one seed, they got the first round off). Then they disman-
tled the Indianapolis Colts 24–14 in the AFC championship. The
opening line on Super Bowl XXXVIII had the Pats giving seven
points to the Panthers.

For the first time in four appearances, the Pats were favorites in
the Super Bowl.

It's easy to be a believer in a season like 2003–04. It's easy to
jump on the bandwagon and let the momentum carry you all the
way to the Super Bowl. But my response to the 2003–04 Patriots
was not a simple matter of a ride on the bandwagon. It was, in
fact, like nothing I've ever experienced with any Pats team. I've
been excited every time the Patriots have played in a Super Bowl.
I've happily rooted for them—against the Bears, the Packers, and
the Rams—but I've done it all without believing. I've done it
with the expectation that the Pats would end Super Bowl Sunday
as the NFL runners up. This time, I did believe. Not just in the
squad of the moment but in the team itself. And I continue to believe. I believe that barring some combination of key injuries, the
team should be back for Super Bowl XXXIX. And maybe Super
Bowl XL, too.

It's foolish to start talking about dynasties after two championships (which really ought to be impressive enough on its own
anyhow), so I won't talk about a dynasty. But I will say that it
would be impossible not to feel good about this team, regardless
of what it's foolish to think or say. And I feel better about this
team than I have about any sports franchise I've cared about since
things turned sour for the Celtics.

I spent Super Bowl Sunday with my old friend Tom and his
girlfriend, Pam, at Tom's house in Douglas. I hadn't been to Tom's
for a game all season. In fact, I hadn't watched a game with anyone other than Seamus (who doesn't really know that much about
football yet) and my wife (who still doesn't care about football)
all season.

It didn't exactly take me by surprise that I wasn't the only person whose larger view of the Patriots had changed during the season, but the change was striking nonetheless.

When I arrived at Tom's an hour and a half before game time, we didn't talk about whether the Pats could win as we had before each of their previous Super Bowl appearances. We didn't even talk about whether the Pats would win. We talked about how they'd win. Both Tom and Pam, like Gainer, were expecting the close game we ended up getting. But neither of them told me I was crazy for predicting a blowout. And even hypothetical talk of a Panthers upset was limited.

"Carolina's a good team," Tom offered at one point.

"I agree," I said. "They were definitely the best team in the NFC."

"They could win."

"Anybody could win. But they'd have to have a lot of things go their way. The Patriots would have to make some mistakes."

"I don't think the Patriots will make mistakes. They don't make a lot of mistakes."

"Right. So the Pats win it."

"Yeah. The Pats win it."

Just as mundane as that. Because there was no reason to get nervous. There was no reason to spend a lot of time thinking about the Panthers and their chances. Not because the Pats were so dominant that they couldn't lose, but because they were so dedicated, so hard working, so determined, that we all knew they'd find a way to win.

The difference between the team we were sitting down to watch that day and the one we'd watched fall to Green Bay on a rainy afternoon 15 months earlier was immeasurable. Not on paper, perhaps. But certainly on the field.

Dave, who was there in Douglas to watch that sorry, muddy loss to the Packers, tells me his experience of the 2003–04 season was much the same as mine. He started paying attention around the time the team's winning streak started, too, doing so, as much of New England did, on the heels of another heartbreaking finish by the Red Sox.

"By the time the Red Sox's season ended, the Pats were 2–2 with Tennessee, the Giants and Miami on the horizon. They had just lost to the Redskins. And I wasn't thinking Super Bowl," Dave told me the week after the Pats beat the Panthers. He came around to believing in the Pats slowly as the season progressed but didn't become a true believer until January. "After they beat the Titans in the play-offs, I was convinced they would win the Super Bowl."

Keith, the guy with whom I'd watched the Pats mount a big comeback victory against the Bears, one of the highlights of the 2002 season, was at the Super Bowl, just as he'd been at Super Bowl XXXVI. The experience, he says, was completely different. He didn't get choked up this time like he did when the Pats beat the Rams.

"There really is nothing like your first championship," Keith says.

I say there's also a difference between winning your first in a major upset (the Pats were two-touchdown underdogs to the Rams in Super Bowl XXXVI) and winning the second as the favorite.

As Keith discovered, there's also a difference in the way you handle the victory as a fan. After Super Bowl XXXVI, he celebrated without reserve in front of the shocked Rams fans. It was a pleasure to do it, given how cocky Rams fans had been in the week leading up to the game. After Super Bowl XXXVIII, he tried to apply some of the lessons he'd learned from interacting with Packers fans the night after Super Bowl XXXI.

"They approached me after the game and said smugly, 'Good game, but the best team won.'" he recalls. "I told them to screw, especially as it got later on Bourbon Street."

He kept that in mind when encountering Panthers fans in Houston in the hours following Super Bowl XXXVIII.

"A few of my buddies gave them the 'good game' line, and I told them to stop," he says.

Hearing something like that makes me glad. While I know Keith is a particularly nice and thoughtful guy, I'm choosing to believe, for now at least, that he was typical of Pats fans who were in Houston for the Super Bowl. I'm choosing to believe that, like the team, the majority of Pats fans still have their heads in the right place— that two championships have not led them to forget what it's like to be on the losing side of the Super Bowl. I know human nature well enough to know I'm kidding myself, but I'm doing it anyway. Because for once in my life I'm letting myself feel good about the Pats. And I'm not interested in spoiling that feeling just yet.

Don, like me, has high hopes for the near future. He's still a Washington Redskins fan first, just as I'm still a Raiders fan first, but he's behind the Pats. And confident that he won't get stung.

Don told me about watching the 2003–04 Pats play, growing more and more confident as the weeks and games went by. "I'm looking at the injury list, seeing multiple starters out every week, Tedy Bruschi playing like his shoes were on fire, [free-agent nose tackle] Ted Washington—I thought he'd retired—the old brick wall he used to be," Don says. "And all I kept thinking was: If these guys are this good now, what are they going to be like when their guys get off the MASH unit?"

For the most part, that question remains unanswered. The Pats were healthier than they'd been all season heading into Super Bowl XXXVIII, but they were still missing some key players, notably the outstanding former Bears linebacker Roosevelt Colvin, who was lost for the season after two games and whose return in September 2004 could make one of the league's best defenses even better. With some room under the NFL's salary cap, a good field of free-agent running backs to pick from, and two picks in each of the first two rounds of a talent-rich 2004 draft ahead of them, the outlook for the Pats in the weeks following Super Bowl XXXVIII couldn't have been better.

Of course, nothing is forever. There will come a time when it's impossible to believe in the Patriots. It may come in 2004 or it may not come until 2014. It may last only a season or two. But that time will certainly come around. That's the way the NFL works.

There will be seasons when the only thing I'll be able to believe is that the Pats are headed for a good pick in the draft. I don't consider that manner of thinking a betrayal, nor even a show of faithlessness. It's simply a practical outlook. No team can be perfect forever; they're all bound to disappoint their fans at some point.

What's different now for the team is that those down periods will never again be all there's ever been. What's different for me is that I'm okay knowing there will be ups and downs. I've learned to relate to the Pats the way I've always related to the Raiders, to accept the hardships of the odd 2–14 season and the vagaries of the all-too-common 9–7 or 8–8 years as necessary trade-offs for the glory of the 14–2 finishes, the magic of the Super Bowl seasons. I've learned not to expect heartbreak year in and year out—and, more important, to accept it when it comes.

I didn't get here on my own. The Pats brought me to this point, but not just by winning Super Bowl XXXVI and Super Bowl XXXVIII. Those big wins were part of it, but so was watching the Pats struggle through the season in between, allowing the team to infuriate me one week only to win my heart again the next, and discovering in the process that it's possible to love the Pats even when I know they may let me down. It's possible because I know, as a team and as an organization, that they want to win, they want to be on top, they want to earn my respect and admiration. And just knowing they want it is enough, even when they don't deliver.

I was also won over by the Pats fans I spent time with during the 2002 season. Not all of them. But the ones who mattered: Louis and Kerrie, Shannon and Keith, my oldest friends, and an assortment of complete strangers. They showed me that you become a fan not just for the team but for the community. You become a fan because it makes you part of something. And you become a fan of the home team because it gives you a connection to the fans who live next door to you, to the fans you grew up with, and to the fans in your office.

I'll never stop being a Raiders fan. I've formed a bond with that team that's too much a part of me to let go. But I've found a way to truly love the Patriots, too. I'm not sure I'd call myself a real Patriots fan (you can only be a real fan of one team per sport), but I would call myself a true believer. A season-in, season-out kind of believer. The team has earned my faith.

It feels good to believe. It feels better to want to believe. And better still to know I can believe without reservation, because in the end, I'm believing in neither a guaranteed winner nor a sure loser; what I believe in is the idea of a team that will try every week of every season to play its best and deliver something meaningful to its fans. It feels good to be along for that ride. It feels good on a February evening, when the Pats have won the league championship. And, more important, it feels good even in the freezing cold of a late-December evening when hope is nothing more than a chimera.

Heartbreak may still be inevitable, but I can live with that. And for now I feel privileged to have a chance to live without it.

About the Author

Sean Glennon is a freelance journalist and a rabid football fan who lives in Florence, Massachusetts with his wife, Maureen Turner, and son, Seamus.

In addition to football, Glennon writes about indie music, sequential art, books, television and pop culture. He is a regular contributor to the Boston Globe and the Journal News (White Plains, New York). And his writing has appeared in such journals as the Boston Phoenix, the Valley Advocate, the Hartford Courant and Salon.com.